Writing Sc

How Scotland's writers
Shaped the Nation

Writing Scotland:
How Scotland's Writers Shaped the Nation

Carl MacDougall

First published in Great Britain in 2004 by
Polygon (an imprint of Birlinn Ltd)
West Newington House
10 Newington Road
Edinburgh
EH9 1QS

www.birlinn.co.uk

ISBN 1 904598 23 4

Scottish
Arts Council
The publishers acknowledge subsidy from the
Scottish Arts Council towards the publication of this volume.

British Library Cataloguing-in-Publication Data
A catalogue record for this book is
available on request from the British Library

Typeset by Hewer Text, Edinburgh
Printed and bound by
Creative Print and Design, Ebbw Vale, Wales

For John
Ring them bells
Bob Dylan

Contents

Sources and Copyright Acknowledgements

Neal Ascherson: from *Stone Voices: The Search for Scotland* (Hill & Wang, 2004) by permission of the author; George Mackay Brown: from 'Beachcomber' from *Selected Poems 1954–1983* (John Murray, 1991) by permission of Hodder Murray; Carol Ann Duffy: 'The Way My Mother Speaks' from *The Other Country* (Anvil Press Poetry, 1990); G. F. Dutton: 'clach eanchainn' from *The Bare Abundance: Selected Poems 1970–2001* (Bloodaxe Books, 2002) by permission of the publisher; Ronald Frame: from *Paris: Play* (Faber & Faber, 1987); Diana Gabaldon: from *Cross Stitch* (Arrow, 1992); Edward Gaitens: from *Dance of the Apprentices* (Canongate Books, 1990); Lewis Grassic Gibbon: from *Sunset Song* (1932), reprinted in *A Scots Quair* (Jarrolds, 1946; Penguin Modern Classics, 1986), The Estate of Mrs J. Leslie Mitchell, by permission of Rhea Martin; W. S. Graham: from 'The Ballad of Baldy Bane' from *Collected Poems 1942–1977* (Faber & Faber, 1979), The Estate of W. S. Graham, by permission of Margaret Snow, Literary Executor; Alasdair Gray: from *Lanark: A Life in Four Books* (Canongate Books, 2002); Tracey Herd: from 'The Siege' from *No Hiding Place* (Bloodaxe Books, 1996) by permission of the publisher; Violet Jacob: from 'The Lang Road' from *Songs of Angus* (John Murray, 1915) by permission of Hodder Murray; Kathleen Jamie: from 'The Queen of Sheba' from *Mr and Mrs Scotland Are Dead: Poems 1980–1994* (Bloodaxe Books, 2002) by permission of the publisher; James Kelman: from *How Late It Was, How Late* (Secker & Warburg, 1994); Harry Lauder: from 'That's The Reason Noo I Wear A Kilt' (1908); Tom Leonard: from 'Unrelated Incidents' from *Intimate Voices* (Etruscan Books, 2003) by permission of the author; Eric Linklater: from *Sealskin Trousers* from *Sealskin Trousers and Other Stories* (Hart-Davis, 1947), Estate of Eric Linklater 1947, by permission of Peters Fraser & Dunlop Group (*www.pfd.co.uk*) on behalf of The Estate of Eric Linklater; Norman MacCaig: from 'The Patriot', from 'My Last Word on Frogs', from 'Dead Friend', from 'November night, Edinburgh', from 'Celtic Cross' and from 'Hugh MacDiarmid' by permission of Polygon (an imprint of Birlinn Ltd); Guy McCrone: from

Wax Fruit (Constable, 1948); **Hugh MacDiarmid**: from 'Gairmscoile', from 'On a Raised Beach', from 'The Glen of Silence', from 'A Drunk Man Looks at the Thistle', from 'Lament for the Great Music' and from 'Empty Vessel' from *Complete Poems: Volume 1* (Carcanet Press, 1993), *Volume 2* (Carcanet Press, 1994) by permission of the publisher; **Duncan Ban Macintyre**: from 'Moladh Beinn Dóbhrain'/'Ben Dorian', translated by Iain Crichton Smith, from *Collected Poems* by Iain Crichton Smith (Carcanet Press, 1992) by permission of the publisher; **Compton Mackenzie**: from *The Monarch of the Glen* (Chatto & Windus, 1941), *1941* by Compton Mackenzie, by permission of The Society of Authors as the Literary Representative of the Estate of Compton Mackenzie; **Sorley MacLean**: from 'Hallaig' from 'An Cuillin' and from 'Palach' from *From Wood to Ridge: Collected Poems in Gaelic and English* (Carcanet Press, 1989) by permission of the publisher; **Kevin MacNeil**: from 'Seahorses' from *Love and Zen in the Outer Hebrides* (Canongate Books, 1998); **Gerald Mangan**: from 'Glasgow 1956' from *Waiting for the Storm* (Bloodaxe Books, 1990); **Elma Mitchell**: 'Comparative Religion' from *The Human Cage* (Peterloo Poets, 1979) by permission of the publisher; **Edwin Morgan**: from 'The Second Life' and from 'Glasgow Sonnets' from *Collected Poems* (Carcanet Press, 1996), and from 'Altus Prosator'/ 'The Maker on High' by St Columba, translated by Edwin Morgan, from *Collected Translations* (Carcanet Press, 1996) by permission of the publisher; **Andrew O'Hagan**: from *Our Fathers* (Faber & Faber, 2000); **Alastair Reid**: 'Scotland' from *Weathering* (Canongate Books, 1978); **Iain Crichton Smith**: from 'Listen', from 'Crofter's Wife', from 'Shall Gaelic Die?', from 'Putting Out The Ashes' and from 'When They Reached The New Land' from *Collected Poems* (Carcanet Press, 1996) by permission of the publisher; **William Soutar**: from 'Owre the Hill' by Walter de la Mare, translated by William Soutar, from *Collected Poems*, edited by Hugh MacDiarmid (Andrew Dakers, 1948) by permission of the Trustees of the National Library of Scotland; **Muriel Spark**: from *The Portobello Road* (Penguin Books, 1995), from *The Ballad of Peckham Rye* (Penguin Books, 1963) and from *The Prime of Miss Jean Brodie* (Penguin Books, 1969); **Alexander Trocchi**: from *Cain's Book* (Calder, 1963).

Every effort has been made to contact all copyright holders. The publisher wishes to apologise if any material has been included without the appropriate acknowledgement, and will be pleased to rectify any omissions or errors brought to their notice at the earliest opportunity.

Preface

Writing Scotland is a major eight-part television series, made by Hopscotch Films for BBC Scotland. The series stems from a core belief that Scotland's unique and distinctive writing tradition has continuously defined the nation, established its identity and was the springboard upon which devolution was built.

For almost 1,500 years Scottish writers have pursued a series of constants and bequeathed a body of literature which is the birth-right of every Scot. They have conferred a wonderful inheritance.

Scottish literature has been our most vibrant export, spreading our ideas and a vision of our country and ourselves across the world. Our range of voices, sense of place and the mythologies we've created continue to tell the world who we are and what made us this way. They have maintained our identity in the face of indifference and defeat, and have made our concerns universal.

Scottish writing has continually highlighted and questioned our social and economic divisions, with Burns' *A Man's a Man* forming a testimony which has inspired our writers ever since its publication. And while our relationship with God and religion has been a continuing factor in the development of our nation's literature, the vision of Scotland many writers took with them when they left has shown us new ways of looking at the familiar, while enriching world literature.

We have a literature of which any country in the world would be proud to boast. In Robert Burns we have one of the world's most celebrated poets. Sir Walter Scott invented the historical and romantic novels, Conan Doyle gave us the world's most famous detective and Robert Louis Stevenson invented the psychological novel. James Hogg's *Memoirs and Confessions of a Justified Sinner* could be placed alongside any masterwork of world literature, Hugh MacDiarmid was one of the greatest European writers of the

20th century and Dame Muriel Spark is surely a candidate for the Nobel laureateship.

One cannot help but wonder why it has taken so long for us to celebrate something which ought to be part of our national life. And why we still see ourselves in terms of something else; why we bother with comparison. It's easy to forget the battles that were fought and in some quarters are still being fought to shake us out of our own complacencies, to try to get us to look at ideas other than our own, to wrench us away from being what we never were, from gentility and standardisation, of a right and proper, maybe even a nice, way of doing things. We need to see ourselves as others see us.

Carl MacDougall
September 2004

Acknowledgements

The *Writing Scotland* series would never have been made without John Archer's energy and enthusiasm. In acknowledging his role as originator and producer, the commitment, help, advice and criticism of the executive producers Clara Glynn and Ewan Angus (for the BBC) were vital. As was the thoughtful care and concern of the directors Angus Cameron, Sarah Barclay and Paul Murton, the Hopscotch staff – especially production manager Arlene Jeffrey and the series researchers David Torbet, David Murdoch, Graeme Burnet and Jenny Niven – and, of course, my companions on the road, the film crew of Neville Kidd, Douglas Kerr and Francis MacNeil.

I would also like to thank the dozens of writers who agreed to be interviewed and who allowed us to use their work. The good news is that Scottish writing has never been healthier, nor its condition more buoyant. For every writer we interviewed there were twice as many waiting in the wings.

And by my sangs the rouch auld Scots I ken
E'en herts that ha'e nae Scots'll dirl richt thro'
As nocht else could – for here's a language rings
Wi datchie sesames, and names for nameless things
From *Gairmscoile* Hugh MacDiarmid

A Sense of Place

Country: Scotland. What like is it?
It's a peat bog, it's a daurk forest.
It's a cauldron o' lye, a saltpan or a coalmine.
It's a bricht bere meadow or a park o' kye.
Or mibbe . . . it's a field o' stanes.
It's a tenement or a merchant's ha'.
It's a hure hoose or a humble cot.
Princes Street or Paddy's Merkit.
                    From *Mary Queen of Scots Got*
                    Her Head Chopped Off Liz Lochhead

How could our landscape not be important? The Highlands have been a running political sore for centuries and are so familiar that even city dwellers see their hills as home. Our sense of place is so strong it's difficult to tell if we inhabit the landscape or if it inhabits us.

Ownership is important. We may feel we own it, instinctively believe it belongs to us, emotionally if not directly:

> This is my country
> The land that begat me.
> These windy spaces
> Are surely my own.
> And those who here toil
> In the sweat of their faces
> Are flesh of my flesh
> And bone of my bone.
>   From *Scotland* Sir Alexander Gray

Owning and belonging are two separate things. The late John McEwen created a stir almost thirty years ago when his detailed study *Who Owns Scotland?* demonstrated that most of the country was in the hands of a few hundred private landowners. Twenty years later the momentum for land reform to be among the new Scottish Parliament's first pieces of legislation could be traced to McEwen's influence. In 1996 the Duke of Buccleuch, the Duke of Atholl, Captain Alwyn Farquharson, the Duchess of Westminster and the Earl of Seafield were among Scotland's top ten landowners with 750,000 acres between them. The Forestry Commission headed the list with more than twice that amount.

Scotland's landowners have, in the main, survived by power, patronage and marriage. They have courted and been wooed by successive governments and exercise unreasonable power on thousands of people and hundreds of communities. Successive studies have shown their land is often poorly managed.

> Who possesses this landscape? –
> The man who bought it or
> I who am possessed by it?
>> From *A Man in Assynt* Norman MacCaig

The notion of belonging is never far from Norman MacCaig. Place, then, involving both geography and history, is something someone else may own but to which we belong. And with place comes a voice, a badge of individual identity as distinctive as a fingerprint.

But the fact that a private landlord, and clan chief, can put the Cuillins up for sale, or that national parks have to be created to preserve what used to be known as the Mar Estate and the area around Loch Lomond, which had effectively become a Glasgow park outside the city boundary, suggests our attachment may be romantic.

Sir Walter Scott used the Highland landscape as a place where people were challenged. It was a wilder, stranger place than they were familiar with. By freeing the landscape of its history, by making it less subjective, emancipated from religion, war, strife and political ideals, it became a place where romance and adventure abounded, where free-spirited men lived simple, untamed lives. It became more attractive and therefore more communitarian. People wanted to identify with the ideals the landscape appeared to embody.

And paintings such as *Loch Maree* by the Glasgow artist Horatio McCulloch, born in the Gallowgate and named after Nelson, are part of the transition of Scottish art into a native landscape, a movement that in many ways was an extension of, and a response to, the novels of Sir Walter Scott. McCulloch's landscape seems exaggerated. Rocks and hills, the sky and water dominate the scene. The only living creatures are the hairy cattle and the only evidence of humanity is the lochside scattering of cottages; another house is tucked away to the left. This is still the spot where bus drivers stop to let passengers photograph the view.

There are no sheep and no people. This is a landscape without people. In this context, McCulloch's use of cattle is interesting. Sheep had previously represented an Arcadian landscape, but the Highland Clearances had altered that perception.

> that great stone
> the shape of a brain
> twisted and left there
>
> out on the moor,
> crystals and fire
> fisted within it,
>
> often has seen
> forests go down
> their soil squandered,

seeds blown in
blown out again,
ashes and iron

beneath it surrendered.
it was begun
with the first star

is now a stone
sheltering foxes
out on the moor.

often have men
marched through the dawn
to give it a name.

clach eanchainn G.F. Dutton

McCulloch's picture was painted in 1866, the year before his death. And two years later, in 1868, Thomas Annan was commissioned by the Glasgow City Improvement Trust to record their work. He photographed back courts and vennels, the tenements and their inhabitants. He was supposed to record the High Street, Saltmarket, Trongate and Gallowgate buildings which were about to be destroyed. But the photographs go beyond historical record. They are composed to make them aesthetically pleasing, particularly in the way objects are placed, people are positioned and the way light comes into the wynds and closes. This gives the pictures an ambiguous quality, which removes them from their historical context, leaving contemporary viewers both delighted by what they see and appalled by the conditions in which the pictures were taken.

Shrill the fife, kettle the drum,
My Queens, my Sluts, my Beauties
Show me your rich attention

Among the shower of empties.
And quiet be as it was once
It fell on a night late
The muse has felled me in this bed
That in the wall is set.
Lie over to me from the wall or else
Get up and clean the grate.

From *The Ballad of Baldy Bane* W.S. Graham

Annan's photographs are a world away from Loch Maree. His pictures are either crowded with people or there is ample evidence of their existence. The people who left the wild, romantic, empty Highlands were either put on boats, shifted to the shore and left to fend for themselves, or they came to places like this and lived in the conditions recorded by Annan.

What place did they envisage? Where did they belong? The area around the High Street absorbed Irish as well as Highland immigrants. We can imagine how they settled. Their battlelines are still being drawn and the old feuds are played out when their football teams meet. When you change one poverty for another, the place is unimportant. And whether their dreams were the same or even similar to those of the people shoved on emigrant ships becomes irrelevant in the face of the need for a new history:

From the lone shieling of the misty island
Mountains divide us, and the waste of the seas –
Yet still the blood is strong, the heart is Highland,
And we in dreams behold the Hebrides.

From *The Canadian Boat Song* Anon

Gaelic-speaking settlers in Canada both preserved the culture they'd carried there and became Canadian. They had been shunted to a place they felt was free and just in ways the Scotland they had left never could be.

My only country
is six feet high
and whether I love it or not
I'll die
for its independence.
The Patriot Norman MacCaig

You could say that Scotland is an illusion, comprising the things we know and hold in our minds. It's the landscape, people, history and culture we customise and call our own. No landscape in Scotland is innocent of its past. Nor can we separate a voice from its location. They are as dependent upon each other as in a Western movie. But its place, the characteristic of belonging that comes from communal identity: that has been the springboard into our sense of ourselves and our identity as a nation.

Writers like Norman MacCaig and George Mackay Brown respect landscape. Their work often openly celebrates the natural rhythms of the seasons and characterises the people who inhabit the places they describe. Yet their approach is different.

MacCaig knew why the Sutherland landscape was barren and though Highland depopulation became an issue for him, it's his experience of the place rather than its history that informs his work.

George Mackay Brown celebrated Orkney and its ways of life. The crofter, equally dependent on land and sea, was symbolic of an existence as old as the place itself. He skips generations like a stone over water. In the late 1960s, he wrote:

Farmers and crofters were poor a generation ago, but their poverty was not like urban poverty. They had as little money as the poor of Glasgow; their wealth was in their few acres and animals and children. There was always meat and drink in a farmhouse – the bere bannocks and butter, the dried cuithes, the white cheese and home-brewed ale – and towards strangers a hospitality almost boundless.

The fishermen sold their haddocks along the street in the nineteen-thirties at threepence a pound. If anything, they were even poorer, living in their little houses above the harbour water, with nothing between them and hunger, between them and drowning, but a yawl.

From An Orkney Tapestry George Mackay Brown

The inhabitants of Skara Brae could easily have lived this way. There was, therefore, something to be learned from history, it offered an existence, maybe even a routine worth preserving, which contemporary society could only threaten and ultimately destroy.

These approaches are as different from the popular concept of place as it's possible to be, and maybe even go some way towards explaining the power of place in Scotland.

Now it is the peculiar character of Scottish as distinct from all other scenery on a small scale in north Europe, to have these distinctively 'mindable' features. One range of coteau [sic] by a French river is exactly like another; one turn of glen in the Black Forest is only the last turn returned; one sweep of Jura pasture and crag, the mere echo of the fields and crags of ten miles away. But in the whole course of Tweed, Teviot, Gala, Tay, Forth, and Clyde, there is perhaps scarcely a bend of ravine, or nook of valley, which would not be recognisable by its inhabitants from every other. And there is no other country in which the roots of memory are so entwined with the beauty of nature, instead of the pride of men; no other in which the song of 'Auld lang syne' could have been written – or Lady Nairne's ballad of 'The Auld Hoose'.

From Landscape and the Seeing Eye John Ruskin

Scottish writers rarely celebrate a landscape simply for its beauty or familiarity. Duncan Ban Macintyre, the Glen Orchy gamekeeper turned Edinburgh policeman, a member of the crew Robert Fergusson called the 'black banditti', does both:

> An t-urram thar gach beinn
> Aig Beinn Dobhrain;
> De na chunnaic mi fo 'nghrein,
> 'S I bu bhoidhche leam:
> Munadh fada reidh,
> Cuilidh 'm faighte feidh,
> Soilleireached an r-sleibh
> Bha mi sonrachadh.

> Honour past all bens
> To Ben Dorian.
> Of all beneath the sun
> I adore her.
> Mountain ranges clear
> storehouse of the deer,
> the radiance of the moor
> I've observed there.
>
> From *Ben Dorian* Duncan Ban Macintyre

Macintyre's great descriptive verses were composed when he worked on the Breadalbane estate and walked the hills of Glen Orchy and Glen Etive, as far as Glen Lochay. They have the immediacy and familiarity of belonging. His poem in praise of Ben Dorian celebrates the gracefulness of the deer the dogs drag down from the hills. The grass and streams are analysed with a near scientific intensity and celebrated because they are his, because he knows them. He is oblivious to history or its impact. But his verse isn't purely descriptive. It is a poetry of belonging more usually found in traditional song, a feature that's lost when a tradition is broken.

Sutherland became Norman MacCaig's spiritual home. He celebrated the landscape and wildlife just as he celebrated and admired the people who inhabited the place, the survivors, those who remained. This was contrasted with the urban confusion of Edinburgh, where he lived for most of the year.

Many of MacCaig's finest poems celebrate wildlife in its natural surroundings. He discovers the same things over and again, finding magic in the ordinary, and gently, often with perfectly placed metaphors and similes, nudges the reader towards his way of seeing. 'Stop looking like a purse,' he tells a toad that clambers towards him like a Japanese wrestler. A heron steps forward like an aunty, a thornbush is an encyclopaedia of angles, straws are scattered like tame lightnings and frogs are everywhere:

> . . . I love
> the elegant way they jump and
> the inelegant way they land.
> So human.

From *My Last Word on Frogs* Norman MacCaig

The poet and novelist Jackie Kay is not alone in being captivated by MacCaig's vision. 'You can never look at a toad in the same way again,' she says, 'and that to me is what really wonderful poets do, they make you look at something like a toad, and they make you see a toad completely differently. Forever and always, toads are purses, and purses are toads.'

Douglas Dunn edited a selection of MacCaig's poetry and suggests his work was a way of explaining the world to himself. 'I think Norman had a gift for contemplating what he observed. He didn't just see it. What is it William Blake said? "As a man sees, so a man is."'

MacCaig's poems are always close to home. They come from more than observation. They originate in his private life and his engagement with people. He is a passionate outsider. His love poems have a restraint that suggests more than privacy is at stake; and the poems he writes about his friends, especially the pieces about MacDiarmid and a friend from Assynt, Angus MacLeod, show an admiration and grief that borders on agony:

How do I meet
a man who's no longer there?
How can I lament the loss
of a man who won't go away?
How can I be changed
by changelessness?

From *Dead Friend* Norman MacCaig

He is rarely directly political; and he always gives the impression that party politics bored him, insofar as they were irrelevant to what he thought and felt. But his feelings about the land and the ways in which it has been separated from the people, both in Edinburgh and Assynt, together with his gift for observation emerge in a complex political and philosophical credo. MacCaig's politics are most easily expressed in the act of choosing; the fact that he writes about a subject suggests sympathy and understanding.

'You get this wonderful playful delight in what he's seeing,' says Douglas Dunn. 'I think what it amounts to in terms of meaning is affection and a sense of it being significant; and a sense also of it being possible to be in harmony with it. He talked of being a Zen Calvinist. I asked if I could join, and he said no.'

The night tinkles like ice in glasses.
Leaves are glued to the pavement with frost.
The brown air fumes at the shop windows,
Tries the doors, then sidles past.

From *November Night, Edinburgh* Norman MacCaig

Dunn suggests MacCaig was the major Scottish poet of the twentieth century, because of the way he refined and simplified his poetry, made his observations clearer. MacCaig's poetry, he says, is 'full of delight, love, decency, wit and wisdom'.

The stone remains . . . to let us know
Their unjust, hard demands, as symbols do.
From *Celtic Cross* Norman MacCaig

Missionary saints incorporated the traditions they found so that the function of holy places remained. Sites that had been used for worship were occupied for Christian use, and from St Ninian's church in Whithorn to St Magnus' Cathedral in Kirkwall, Scotland is rich in places where one faith has been inherited from another.

The very names suggest their function. Places beginning with the prefix 'Kil' mark the location of a church, a monastery or place of worship. But it's more usual to find relics that are obviously significant, that are carefully sited and seem to be part of a sacred landscape, where their meaning or function can scarcely be guessed. For writers these places symbolise the mystery of endurance.

Nearby the bit loch was a circle of stones from olden times, some were upright and some were flat and some leaned this way and that, and right in the middle three big ones clambered up out of the earth and stood askew with flat sonsy faces, they seemed to listen and wait.
From *Sunset Song* Lewis Grassic Gibbon

Aristotle believed the earth was eternal, existing for all time. But, using Old Testament references, in 1664, Bishop Ussher of Armagh concluded the earth was made at nine o'clock in the morning of 26 October, 4004 BC.

Scotland has the oldest rocks in Europe. The Stoer group in Sutherland, well known to Norman MacCaig, that stretches into the North Minch were deposited 995 million years ago, and are among the oldest anywhere.

The landscape of Kilmartin, near Oban, is littered with evidence of our ancestors. People have occupied this place for something like 10,000 years. It's reckoned some of these prehistoric monuments represent a struggle to fix time accurately by reference to the sun and moon. Fifteen hundred years ago, 'A line of at least seven cairns dominated the valley floor,' it says in the guidebook. 'Standing stones – some single, some in complex arrangements – dotted the landscape, and rock carvings decorated view points and access ways. Precious objects were placed in the cairns in the valley and in stone built graves on gravel terraces at the valley edges.'

These must be amongst our first man-made objects, offering a gateway into history:

The inward gates of a bird are always open
It does not know how to shut them
That is the secret of its song,
But whether any man's are ajar is doubtful.
I look at these stones and know little about them,
But I know their gates are open too,
Always open, far longer open, than any bird's can be.

From *On a Raised Beach* Hugh MacDiarmid

MacDiarmid was a publicist and politician as well as one of our greatest poets. He opened the twentieth-century language debate in Scotland, launching what he called the Scottish Renaissance Movement. Scotland was a weapon in his struggle to write good poetry. He used standing stones to symbolise the purity of the ancient Scottish race and made them a basis for his vision of national identity. Like many other writers, he was fascinated by the continuity of human experience the stones evoked.

Neal Ascherson grew up in Kilmartin and has known the stones all his life. When his mother was ill in hospital in Oban, he passed them every day, driving from 'the small house to which its owner would never return'. They took on a new significance.

There are many kinds of revelation. But the most powerful is the vision which transcends the mental boundary between life and non-life, and Scotland is a place where this sort of revelation often approaches. Staring into a Scottish landscape, I have often asked myself why – in spite of all appearances – bracken, rocks, man and sea are at some level one. Sometimes this secret seems about to open, like a light moving briefly behind a closed door.

From Stone Voices Neal Ascherson

He sees the stones as 'barbs sticking into the fish of time, trying to hold it back and remind you of something. Stones have a life, these stones have a biography like human beings.'

Parts of the biography are chipped or rubbed into them. Different uses, mythical or practical, that humans have devised can be read or inferred; much of it remains unreadable though a surprising amount of biography is simply lying around waiting to be noticed. 'It has remained unstudied because historians and archaeologists have been so exclusively obsessed with an artefact's birth – and have almost ignored its life,' he says.

Neal told me that at the end of one of the walks organised by the Kilmartin House Museum, the guide asked her party of American visitors if they had any questions. A woman said she'd enjoyed the walk and found the talk interesting but wanted to know why they'd put the stones in the middle of a field.

Most Scots can not call up a vision of their landscape which does not bear the mark of man . . . Human settlement and activity are no more than a form of lichen which can take hold in the less exposed crevices and surfaces of the land . . . Much of Scotland's soil is shallow and acid, the rock pokes through worn sleeve of the turf . . . This has been a hard country to live in as in many ways it still is. Scottish earth is a skin over bone and like any taut face it never loses a line once acquired. Seen from the air, every trench dug over the millennia and every dyke raised, every hut footing and post hole, fort bank and cattle path, tractor mark and chariot rut seems to have inscribed its trace.

From Stone Voices Neal Ascherson

Writing of his mother's childhood, at the beginning of the last century, he recalls a time when people made their own clothes, lit their homes with paraffin and walked miles to work or school. 'A boat pushing out into the sea would always be turned sun-wise towards its course; a body taken from the kirk to a grave would be carried sun-wise round the building,' he says.

He could be describing Mackay Brown's Orkney. Brown's work grew from the people who struggled to survive on land and sea. He dedicated his life to this place and rarely left it.

There was something emblematic about him. 'To be so supplicated in your reading and to be intellectually excited by ideas from other writers right around the world yet to live in your own particular place, that I find is particularly Scottish,' says Jackie Kay.

George Mackay Brown constructed a Scotland that was far removed from the modern world, a place with a timeless way of life that was free from what he saw as society's manipulation and control. By delving into the past of one of the world's oldest, remotest and most secluded places he made the landscape, the seasons and the way of life as much a character as inhabitant:

> Monday I found a boot –
> Rust in salt leather.
> I gave it back to the sea, to dance in.
>
> Tuesday a spar of timber worth thirty bob.
> Next winter.
> It will be a chair, a coffin, a bed.
>
> Wednesday a half can of Swedish spirits.
> I tilted my head.
> The shore was cold with mermaids and angels.
> From *Beachcomber* George Mackay Brown

'George Mackay Brown was absolutely dedicated to the notion of Scotland's ancient myths,' says novelist Andrew O'Hagan. 'He believed there was a meaningfulness in those ancient legends, what they meant, what the stones meant, what the land was made of; he was utterly aware of that, and saw rocks in the same way as Hugh MacDiarmid, our ancestors were there, our story was there, the DNA of Scotland was there, and literature's business was to excavate that.'

Orkney for Mackay Brown was a microcosm of the human race. The place of fabulous significance celebrated by Edwin Muir, his Other Eden, became the world to Mackay Brown who studied at Newbattle Abbey under Muir in the early 1950s.

Mackay Brown was prolific. As well as several volumes of poetry, he published five novels, eight short story collections, poem-plays, stories for children, studies of Orkney, a libretto for Peter Maxwell Davies and every Friday's *Orcadian* newspaper carried a column by him. His work intensified Muir's mythology, localising its impact and disguising his intentions with lucid metaphors and images. His work is simply variations on a theme, material progress was at best transient and at worse destructive. Place is more than a land and a people. It is history and, more importantly, it is tradition.

> Wha gangs wi' us owre the hill
> And is baith far and near?
> Abune the bluid that lifts and fa's
> Anither hert we hear.
>> From *Owre the Hill* (by Walter de
>> la Mare) trans. William Soutar

The continuity of place, the mysterious stones and trenches, the mounds that once were hill forts or hidden graves, give certain sites an impact that can often be felt as a presence. Sorley MacLean was not the only writer to carry this feeling to its logical conclusion.

He was Scotland's most celebrated modern Gaelic poet. Born in 1911, he spent most of his life as a schoolteacher and headmaster. He began publishing poetry just before the Second World War and was writing until his death in 1996. He had an international reputation and was nominated for a Nobel Prize. His poems have been translated into many languages. For him the land represented political struggle; a troubled history lying just below the surface.

Despite economic explanation and revisionist histories, the Highland Clearances are an emblematic part of Scotland's political identity. For the best part of 150 years, from around 1750, the Highland people suffered hunger and eviction. Gaelic surnames proliferate in Glasgow and Edinburgh; Scottish place-names are common in America; and it is possible to learn Harris dances and Scottish fiddle styles in Cape Breton. Like most Scottish scars, the Clearances were self-inflicted. And like the others they were motivated by a desire for status and English cupidity.

For centuries drove roads were used to drive the cattle from the Highlands to the trysts at Crieff and Falkirk, then the cities of the south. It was a difficult and hazardous journey for which cattle were shod and could travel no more than a dozen miles a day. No one knows why it should be so, but from the earliest times Scotland was known as a cattle-producing country with the most important supplies coming from the remote areas of western and north-western Scotland, particularly from Skye. Roads made by trotting cattle were later used to transport people.

Sorley MacLean was born and spent his childhood in the small crofting community at Oskaig on Raasay, the setting for his wonderful poem *Hallaig*. He died across the water in Braes. Behind Oskaig are the woods of Raasay and the Cuillins are straight ahead. Both were subjects of his poems.

I walked to Hallaig with the Gaelic poet Aonghas MacNeacail. We'd admired Sorley's poetry for decades, but neither of us had visited the place. Aonghas has no doubts about why Sorley should identify so strongly with Hallaig.

'He was a child of tradition bearers,' he said, 'and when you have that lore, a tradition of songs and stories and pipe tunes that identify with a place, it gives you a very distinctive sense of the place's importance.'

And with the connection came a particular responsibility to keep the village alive, to ensure its memory did not fade. The complexity of a Scottish community is something writers have tried to establish, utilise, develop and celebrate. But none had tried to resurrect.

On a beautiful still day Hallaig evoked a mixture of quiet anger and grief. The sun, warm wind and the lush green of summer made the eviction even more wicked. You could sense the people in the houses; they may no longer be there, but something more than ruins remained. It was in the small things. The earth still packed between the stones on a house wall to keep out the draught; the scrape of the lazybeds; the grass and heather taken root where the thatch had been. It wasn't difficult to imagine the houses occupied, children tumbling down the braes, men and women sitting on the mossy banks. Something stayed when the villagers left. It's clear they were forced out.

One hundred and twenty families were shipped from Hallaig in a single day and this wasn't an isolated event. It was repeated over and over again throughout the Highlands for years.

Tha iad fhathast ann a Hallaig
Clann Ghill-Eain's Clann MhicLeoid,
na bh'ann ri linn Mhic Ghille-Chaluim:
Chunnacas na Mairbh beo.

Na fir 'nan laighe air an lianaig
aig ceann gach taighe a bh' ann,
na h-igheanan 'nan coille bheithe,
direach an druim, crom an ceann.

Eadar la Leac is na Fearnaibh
tha 'n rathad mor fo choinnich chiuin,
's na h-igheanan 'nam badan samhach
a' dol a Chlachan mar o thus.

Agus a tilleadh as a Chlachan,
a Suidhisnis 's a tir nam beo;
a chuile te og uallach
gun bhristeadh cridhe an sgeoil.

They are still in Hallaig
MacLeans and MacLeods,
all who were there in the time of Mac Gille Chaluium
the dead have been seen alive.

The men lying on the green
at the end of every house that was,
the girls a wood of birches,
straight their backs, bent their heads.

Between the Leach and Fearns
the road is under mild moss
and the girls in silent bands
go to Clachan as in the beginning,

and return from Clachan
from Suisnish and the land of the living;
each one young and light-stepping,
without the heartbreak of the tale.

From *Hallaig* Sorley MacLean

Aonghas recognises the anger in the poem: 'But curiously,' he says, 'it's both a eulogy and celebration. He refused to let them die, refused to let their spirit die.'

'The dead have been seen alive' is one of the most staggeringly haunting lines in all Scottish literature. It comes from a poem about the Clearances, where the subject is never mentioned. Events take place 'without the heartbreak of the tale'.

The historian Tom Devine has shown the Clearances weren't just a Highland phenomenon. Between 1760 and 1830 the communities known as *ferm touns* were replaced throughout Scotland by what he called, 'a recognisably modern landscape of trim fields and compact farms, separated by hedges and ditches'.

Common lands were absorbed into the landlord's domain as the cottars who worked them were replaced by farm labourers who fee'd for a term and moved on. A hard-working labourer in the north-east of Scotland could aspire to leasing a croft of his own.

A croft was a small farm of anything up to 100 acres, worked by a tenant and his family. The soil of north-east Scotland was more fertile than that of the west and crofting was neither so bleak nor as varied. Leases were better and crofts were bigger.

In the spring of 1908, James Mitchell took lease of a croft at Bloomfield, two miles above the village of Arbuthnott for an annual rent of £15/3/9. Mitchell arrived with the young wife he'd married ten years earlier, her two sons and their son, James Leslie Mitchell, who was seven years old.

Mitchell's independence came at a price. He was a stern, unemotional man who had little time for books and subjected his family to a remorseless creed of harsh work and discipline. Emigration and the movement of people was an everyday fact in north-east communities. Larger farms encroached on their land. A crofter's priority was to grow crops to feed the family, with cash crops being sold on the open market. A farmer's ambitions were higher than subsistence.

The work meant that his sons had scarcely any childhood, though by the age of ten, Leslie was already the odd one out. The boys attended the village school three miles away. Leslie later calculated he walked over 14,000 miles in search of education. Contemporaries remember him as being absorbed in a book while they were playing, and his step-brothers George and John recalled how he resented spending time away from reading to do his farm chores.

John later wrote, 'There wasn't much in those days, but he made do with whatever there was, anything at all, newspapers, magazines, *The People's Friend*, even the backs of cigarette cards. He could never get enough to satisfy his appetite for books, and his thirst for information . . . And he remembered everything he read or heard. He had a wonderful memory.'

The village community and the Bloomfield croft stayed with him. At night, when lights appeared in houses on the surrounding hills, the place took on an eerie, unexpected beauty, which he later described.

That is The Land out there, under the sleet, churned and pelted there in the dark, the long rigs upturning their clayey faces to the spear-onset of the sleet. That is The Land, a dim vision this night of laggard fences and long stretching rigs. And the voice of it – the true and unforgettable voice – you can hear even in such a night as this as the dark comes down, the immemorial plaint of the peewit, flying lost. That is The Land – though not quite all. Those folk in the byre whose lantern light is a glimmer through the sleet as they muck and bed and tend the kye, and milk the milk into tin pails, in curling froth – they are The Land in as great a measure.

From *The Land* Lewis Grassic Gibbon

The extract is from an essay published in 1934 in *Scottish Scene: or the Intelligent Man's Guide to Albyn*, the book where Lewis Grassic Gibbon collaborated with our other pseudonymous hero, Christopher Murray Grieve, also known as Hugh MacDiarmid. When James Leslie Mitchell created a new identity he took his mother's name. *Scottish Scene* followed his most famous work, *A Scots Quair*.

A Scots Quair was published in three parts annually between 1932 and 1934. Gibbon intended it to be read as a novel. It was conceived as a whole and published as a trilogy to suit the publishers. The first part of the trilogy, *Sunset Song*, is one of Scotland's best-loved books, and was an instant success. Published in August 1932, it was reprinted a further five times before the end of the year.

It's the story of Chris Guthrie's journey from the crofting community of Kinraddie to the squalor and poverty of the industrial city of Duncairn. Chris' connection to the land is central. She survives rape, bereavement and the breakdown of her marriage, but the place she comes from, her sense of belonging, provides her with strength and continuity.

And then a queer thought cam to her there in the drooked fields, that nothing endured at all, nothing but the land she passed across, tossed and turned and perpetually changed below the hands of the crofter folk since the oldest of them had set the Standing Stones by the loch of Blawearie and climbed there on their holy days and saw their terraced crops ride brave in the wind and sun . . . but the land was forever, it moved and changed below you, but was forever, you were close to it and it to you, not at a bleak remove it held you and hurted you. And she had thought to leave it all!

From *Sunset Song* Lewis Grassic Gibbon

The novelist and short story writer Anne Donovan views the sense of place as imperative. 'I think it's one of these books that if you've read it you feel as if you've been here,' she said. 'Actually coming here feels familiar.'

Quair is Scots for book and Gibbon was reflecting in the title his ambitions for the trilogy. He wanted to tell the definitive story of industrial birth. Even the individual titles have meaning: *Sunset* signified the end of the crofting system; *Song* was the Song of Scotland. In the second book in the trilogy, *Cloud Howe*, Chris' husband Robert Colquohoun, anticipating his wife's pregnancy, says, 'Oh Chris Caledonia, I've married a nation!'

The trilogy progresses from the rural scenes of *Sunset Song* to the city scenes of *Grey Granite* and though Gibbon lamented that shift, he also recognised its inevitability. The great loss was that change brought no improvement. It became, for some, another source of wealth. As the people changed to urban proletariat, their material and economic condition stayed the same at best, but was more likely to bring additional hardship. They were still exploited and kept in poverty. The sense of community was gone. The sense of belonging was gone. The city could be anywhere. They had no connection with it or what they produced.

The books were written in Welwyn Garden City. Gibbon had an ambivalent attitude towards the land and the attitude is reflected in his work. He loved and hated it with equal passion. 'You love it and you hate it and you cannae live without it,' says Anne Donovan. 'I believe he had to go away in order to be able to write about it.'

But his ashes are buried in Arbuthnott Cemetery and inscribed at the bottom of his tombstone is a phrase from *Sunset Song*, 'And I will give you the morning star', which comes from one of the most beautiful and poignant parts of the book, where the Reverend Robert Colquohoun gives a speech on the commemoration of the war memorial, which he had commissioned a mason to fashion from a standing stone.

With them we may say there died a thing older than themselves, these were the Last of the Peasants, the last of the Old Scots folk. A new generation comes up that will know them not, except as a memory in a song, they passed with the things that seemed good to them, with loves and desires that grow dim and alien in the days to be. It was the old Scotland that perished then, and we may believe that never again will the old speech and the old songs, the old curses and the old benedictions, rise but with alien effort to our lips. The last of the peasants, those four you knew, took that with them to the darkness and the quietness of the places where they sleep. And the land changes, their parks and their steadings are a desolation where the sheep are pastured, we are told that great machines come soon to till the land, and the great herds come to feed on it, the crofter has gone, the

man with the house and steading of his own and the land
closer to his heart than the flesh of his body.

From Sunset Song Lewis Grassic Gibbon

The end of *Grey Granite*, the last of the *Quair*, finds Chris back in
the countryside where her family lived before they moved to
Blawearie. She finds a vantage point in an old Pictish fort on the
Hill of Fare, where she reflects on her life and its journey:
'Deliverer, Destroyer and Friend in one.' She drops out of history,
leaving the future to others. She returns to the land, to the peesies
and the rain.

Like Gibbon, Neil Gunn drew on his childhood and used it to
create a place where landscape and community are inextricably
linked, by a common past and a present dependence. His people
often have to find their own solutions, but they are connected to
each other and the place by the shared web of the past. Gunn
shows the strengths of these values, when they are challenged by
the worst the twentieth century has to offer.

His starting point is the community. Here he finds his springboard into the past and his hope for the future. He celebrates
Highland myth and tradition, but from a position of regeneration.
Rather than seeing the past as something which had failed the
Highlands, Gunn saw it as a positive force which offered the
possibility of restoring completeness, something he felt was missing in the twentieth century, offering the possibility of regeneration from within. His characters search for personal development,
rather than material improvement, and tend to rely on their own
resources or the resources of their community rather than a social
or political ideal.

Neil Gunn was born in Dunbeath on the Caithness coast, the
fifth of seven boys in a family of nine. His father was a fisherman
and though Gunn was not a Gaelic speaker, he was aware of the
area's traditions, especially its connections with a Pict and Nordic
past.

Gunn's political development was acute. One brother was killed in the First World War, another was badly gassed and the twins who had emigrated to Canada lost their lives as a result of their army service. Gunn worked for the Excise and when he was first married was posted to Wigan where he assessed pension claims of miners who were suffering as a result of the local coal owners' wage cuts and lock outs.

In *Highland River*, Gunn places the experiences of childhood, when a tangible loving relationship is developed with place, at the heart of deliverance from the war and social change. As a result of its success, T.S. Eliot encouraged him to write full-time, and in *The Silver Darlings*, Gunn links personal growth with the decline of the herring industry in the nineteenth century.

Finn grows up without a father. His parents have been forced to the shore by the Clearances.

They had come from beyond the mountain which rose up behind them, from inland valleys and swelling pastures, where they and their people before them had lived from time immemorial. The landlord had driven them from these valleys and pastures, and burned their houses, and set them here against the sea-shore to live if they could and, if not, to die.

From *The Silver Darlings* Neil Gunn

Catrine's inexperienced husband Tormad is press-ganged into the navy and for twenty years his wife doesn't know if he's alive or dead. When he appears in a dream, she comes to terms with his departure and believes he has truly gone from her.

Though she hates the sea and tries to turn her son against it, she becomes acquainted with Roddy Sinclair, the youngest skipper in Dunster. They eventually marry in middle age and produce a child whose ancestry is a mixture of Viking and Celt, producing a new breed of Scot.

Finn's epiphany comes on the night before his wedding when he retreats to a place of sanctuary. His relationship with the land embodies his continual need to withdraw from society to consider what it means.

> By this cold shuddering fir of fear
> My heart divines a presence here,
> Goddess or ghost yclept;
> Wrecker of homes . . .

> Where have I heard a silence before
> Like this that only a lone bird's cries
> And the sound of a brawling burn today
> Serve in this wide empty glen but to emphasise?
>
> From *The Glen of Silence* Hugh MacDiarmid

Many left for the industrial south, to Glasgow, the Lanarkshire steel mills, coal mines and surrounding towns. Not surprisingly, much of the writing reflects a deep suspicion of cities. An older, purer Scotland, morally and linguistically, was found in the countryside.

Violet Jacob's poem *The Lang Road*, written around the start of the First World War, features an old woman thinking about her three sons. Two have died in battle. But it's the one who's still alive, the lad who's living in the city, whom she feels is most distant.

> And far ayont the bit o'sky that lies abune the hills,
> There is the black toon standin' mid the roarin' o' the mills
> Whaur the reek frae mony engines hangs atween it and the
> sun
> And the lives are weary, weary, that are just begun.
>
> From *The Lang Road* Violet Jacob

The Industrial Revolution happened more quickly and brutally here than in many other countries and in the main our writers viewed the change retrospectively. The fact that Glasgow was the hub of the Industrial Revolution seemed to pass our writers by; few documented the effects of industrial transformation.

In his Introduction to *Mungo's Tongues: Glasgow Poems 1630–1990* Hamish Whyte notes a loosely formed côterie of writers gathered in the 1850s, '. . . many of them feeling – as industry tightened its grip on the city, the population grew, living room shrank and the skies darkened – the stark contrast between town and country.'

Ellen Johnston wasn't one of them. By the age of ten she was working as a power-loom weaver. She died in a Glasgow poorhouse before her thirty-ninth birthday. In her poem *The Last Sark*, a woman whose husband is out of work hasn't eaten for three days. There's nothing to pawn but his old blue shirt:

Our merchants and mill-masters they wad never want a meal
Though a' the banks in Scotland wad for a twalmonth fail;
For some o' them hae far mair gowd than ony ane can see.
What care some gentry is they're weel though a' the puir wad
    dee?

From *The Last Sark* Ellen Johnston

James Macfarlan and Alexander Smith were part of the group. Macfarlan died in poverty, aged thirty. Thackeray compared him to Burns and he was published by Dickens. Another poet, James Slimmon, Bard of Kirkintilloch, described him as a 'ragged, unkempt, mean-looking tramp . . . from dingy garrets and common lodging-houses in the slums of Glasgow'. Another states, 'meanness . . . and drink . . . were native to him'. Macfarlan died in 1862 and wrote *The Wanderer* in 1857:

Mighty furnaces are flaring like a demon's breath of fire,
Forges, like great burning cities, break in many a crimson
    spire;
Tongues of eager flame are lapping all the glory of the
    heaven,
While a blush of burning hectic o'er the midnight's face is
    driven.

Peels the thunder throat of labour, hark! the deaf'ning anvils
   clash,
Like a thousand angry sabres in a battle's headlong dash.
Hear the thoroughfares of tumult, like the midnight ocean's
   roar
As in agony he clutches at the black heart of the shore.
Toiling there the poor boy-poet, grimed, within a dismal den,
Piles the fire, and wields the hammer, jostled on by savage
   men;
Burns his life to mournful ashes on a thankless hearth of
   gloom,
For a paltry pittance digging life from out an early tomb.
And the soul is dwarfed within him that was cast in Titan
   mould,
And the wealth of heaven he loses for the lack of human gold,
And he cannot see the stars arise in splendid sheen of light,
Like angel watchfires gleaming on the cloudy cliffs of night!

From *The Wanderer* James Macfarlan

Writers clung to the ideal that cities didn't belong in Scotland. The
legacy of Burns and Scott had been to concentrate our language
and history into small idealised rural communities, despite the fact
that by the middle of the nineteenth century two-thirds of our
population were living in towns and, by 1900, half the population
lived in and around Glasgow.

City! I am true son of thine;
Ne'er dwelt I where great mornings shine
Around the bleating pens;
Ne'er by the rivulets I strayed,
And ne'er upon my childhood weighed
The silence of the glens.
Instead of shores where ocean beats,
I hear the ebb and flow of streets.

From *Glasgow* Alexander Smith

Smith's poem was also written in 1857 and reflects an unusual optimism about city life. It comes from a collection called *City Poems*, and though Smith is aware of his surroundings – 'Wave am I in that sea of woes' – he discerns 'another beauty sad and stern':

> A sacredness of love and death
> Dwells in thy noise and smoky breath.

Edwin Muir felt no such buoyancy.

'I was born before the Industrial Revolution,' he wrote in *The Story and The Fable*, 'and am now about two hundred years old. But I have skipped a hundred and fifty of them. I was really born in 1737, and till I was fourteen no time-accidents happened to me. Then in 1751 I set out from Orkney to Glasgow. When I arrived I found that it was not 1751 but 1901.'

Muir considered Glasgow the most important city in Scotland. 'A description of Scotland which did not put Glasgow at the centre of the picture would not be a description of Scotland at all,' he wrote in *Scottish Journey*. Despite that, his impressions were, 'mostly, I am afraid, painful'.

The move to Glasgow precipitated the death of Muir's parents, two brothers; and his own health suffered. It was more than theory or intellectual posturing that made Muir the perpetual outsider. His experience created a need to belong, to be part of something bigger than himself.

Andrew O'Hagan notes that Muir's early poems describe the move from Orkney as similar to being thrown out of the Garden of Eden. 'In a sense he was exiled,' he says. 'He describes being on the tram in Glasgow and looking at people's eyes moving in their head like animals' eyes.'

There is, he suggests, the sense of a very fine literary intelligence that feels abandoned. 'It feels it's been removed from its natural environment, which was an older Scotland, a Scotland of rocks, lochs, emptiness, into somewhere crushed, pulsating and full.'

Muir's experience made him stare into the reality of Glasgow. He felt the Glasgow slum-dwellers faced a lifetime of imprisonment, a more dreadful punishment than death. He despises the fools who argue about which slums are the worse; those who condemn the people who live there on social, political or religious grounds; and, especially, those who relate tales of their awfulness, playing to an appetite which can never be sated.

Accounts of the Glasgow slums are uniform in their conclusions and it's no surprise that the fictional tone for the city was set by a book whose characters precisely fitted what decent people, living elsewhere, expected of folk who lived in such awful conditions. *No Mean City* has never been out of print since it became the paradigm of Glasgow books. For the best part of a generation its razor slashers and herries typified the city.

It took writers like Edward Gaitens, George Friel, Archie Hind, Robin Jenkins and William McIlvanney to offer a picture of city life that was recognisable to most of the folk who lived there.

There's always a headscarf stooped
into a pram, nodding in time
with a plastic rattle, outside a shop
advertising a sale of wallpaper.

From *Glasgow 1956* Gerald Mangan

The writer who has seen Glasgow through its metamorphosis from mince to lemongrass is Edwin Morgan. From the late 1950s and 1960s, a time when most other writers were despairing of modernism, he displayed a buoyant optimism, not only about Glasgow's modernisation, but also about the people and place itself. The collection which heralded the arrival of a restless, experimental voice was *The Second Life*, published in 1968. A generation of Scottish schoolchildren have been examined on poems from this collection: *King Billy, In the Snack Bar, Glasgow Green, The Starlings in George Square, Trio* and the title poem:

Can it be like this, and is this what it means
in Glasgow now, writing as the aircraft roar
over building sites, in this warm west light
by the daffodil banks that were never so crowded and lavish –
green May, and the slow great blocks rising
under yellow tower cranes, concrete and glass and steel
out of the dour rubble it was and barefoot children gone –

From *The Second Life* Edwin Morgan

Morgan has written science fiction and concrete poems, and he is known as a translator and originator of poetic forms like Instamatic Poems, Newspoems and Poems from the Video Box. He is the writer who comes closest to what it means to be a *makar*, someone who is a craftsman, who makes and shapes and experiments with words and the sound of the voice. From the first, he saw himself as a Glasgow poet, which was unusual: others of his generation were following MacDiarmid's lead and writing for Scotland. He did a little of that, too, but principally he was trying to say something for and do something with the subject of Glasgow.

'I felt there was something important, and attractive and good and human about Glasgow,' he says, 'that had to be written about, particularly round about the Sixties when it was changing so much, very dramatically being changed physically by redevelopment. I felt very strongly that I wanted to write about that.'

Andrew O'Hagan reckons the changing city, 'absolutely transformed [Morgan] as a poet . . . The landscape was being completely altered, the urban spaces were being experimented with and that experimentalism appealed to linguistic experimentalism of a poet in the city like Edwin Morgan.'

Morgan later changed his view about modernism, as did most others. He traded in the shining optimism of the 1960s for a view of Glasgow that was ambivalent and much darker, typifying many Scottish writers. They may love and celebrate a place, but they are acutely aware of its failings. Morgan will not let us look away. This is the second of his *Glasgow Sonnets*:

A shilpit dog fucks grimly by the close.
Late shadows lengthen slowly, slogans fade.
The YY PARTICK TOI grins from its shade
like the last strains of some lost libera nos
a malo. No deliverer ever rose
from these stone tombs to get the hell they made
unmade. The same weans never make the grade.
The same grey street sends back the ball it throws.
Under the darkness of a twisted pram
a cat's eye glitters. Glittering stars press
between the silent chimney-cowls and cram
the higher spaces with their SOS.
Don't shine a torch on the ragwoman's dram.
Coats keep out the evil cold less and less.

From *Glasgow Sonnets* Edwin Morgan

The darker side of city life is often most successfully captured in detective fiction where the formula of using real places in made-up stories has been tried and tested many times. Given the city's reputation, it's surprising more writers haven't exploited the image. Denise Mina lives in Glasgow and *Garnethill* is where her imagination breathes.

Garnethill was Glasgow's second development. Steeper than the grid iron plan of Blythswood New Town on the other side of Sauchiehall Street, it was originally called Summerhill and has always been distinct. Residential development began in the 1820s, but the Garnethill Observatory, opened in 1810, attracted a steady stream of visitors. Thomas de Quincey visited in daylight to view the town rather than the stars: '. . . tarnished with eternal canopies of smoke, and of sorrow, how dark with the agitations of many orders, is the mighty town below!' In comparison, the Observatory was serene, quiet and solemn: 'lifted above the confusion', he wrote. Garnethill's best known building is Charles Rennie Mackintosh's School of Art.

Denise reckons a real place gives the writer a skeleton of truth to hang a lot of lies on very credibly. 'It's a very high area of the town,' she says. 'It's quite isolated. It's isolated because people don't come up here much. The central character lives at the top of a tenement and she's looking down on the city, and slightly apart from it, so that Garnethill symbolised that as well.'

An Edinburgh winter could be a real stayer, starting early in October and lasting into April. These days were not constant: sometimes it was twilight all day; other times, with fresh snow on the ground, the sun's glare scoured your eyes. People walked everywhere squinting, either peering into the gloom or protecting themselves from the fierce light.

Today was a twilight day, the sky a dull maroon, threatening a fall. Rebus stuffed his hands into his pockets and felt the small paper bag. He'd found an ironmonger's on Gorgie Road, and had been directed to a specialist shop where he'd been sold a radiator key. Now he walked around, found the house he was looking for, and walked up to the front door.

From *Let It Bleed* Ian Rankin

Ian Rankin is one of Scotland's most successful writers, having written one in every ten books sold. He was thinking of writing a crime novel when he came across William McIlvanney's *Laidlaw*, about a Glasgow detective. McIlvanney was a respected novelist, who'd won the Whitbread Prize, and, 'At the 1985 Edinburgh Book Festival I went up to him to get my copy of *Laidlaw* signed. I said, "I'm writing a book that's got a Edinburgh detective in it," and he wrote "Good luck with the Edinburgh Laidlaw" on the inside of the book and I've still got it upstairs. It's got pride of place in my library.'

Though he has solved crimes in London and Glasgow, the very fabric of Edinburgh seems to inhabit Rebus. And because his job takes him across the city, the place he inhabits is more than one-dimensional. No other writer has covered the city so well nor in such detail, taking in the contrasts and extremes that define the capital. Yet the early novels were written in France.

Moving abroad meant the books became fiction, in the sense that everything had to be invented. But the geography and, more importantly, the feel of the place was right. Ian came back to Edinburgh once or twice a year to check that the city wasn't changing and he had a number of friends who corresponded regularly, told him the price of a pint, if pub opening hours had changed, how and if it still took the same length of time to go from one place to another, and which buses took certain routes.

Rankin shows us the Edinburgh we know, the tourist place. Then he flips the coin and shows us the other side. Tourists can now take a pint in the Oxford Bar, and then see where Rebus lives and where certain crimes were committed in the Rebus walking tours. This is possible because the books are set in a real place. Having created a fictional Edinburgh in the early books, the old police station, a fictional creation, was burned to the ground and Rebus began to inhabit the real world. New visitors will find that the police station's moved.

'There is no longer a CID at St Leonard's,' says Ian. 'So St Leonard's police station where Rebus has happily worked for the past seven or eight books has had to go and I've had to relocate him.'

Andrew O'Hagan's novel *Our Fathers* also deals with change, loss and disappointment.

When he was growing up, O'Hagan remembers being struck by how the landscape he inhabited was new: 'An old Scotland had a new plan grafted on top, and we were part of that plan. In *Our Fathers* there's a scene where a building's being blown down. The people are all drinking ginger and it's supposed to be a day of celebration; they're blowing down this building in the Gorbals finally realising it didn't work. It was part of an idealism that failed, but as the building's coming down suddenly a silence descends on these people.'

Everything was quiet.

The sadness you feel when a house comes down. You feel for the people who lived there. All those sitting rooms and painted walls, gone in an instant, as if the hours that passed inside meant nothing much, as if they never happened. The shape of those rooms will always remain in the minds of those who lived there. People will grow up with a memory of their high view over Glasgow. The thought of the rooms will bring back conversations, the theme-tunes of television shows; and above all that they will bring back innocence. Life will always be like this, they thought. But what they thought came down with the rumble too. They lived in those rooms, but they will never see them again.

From *Our Fathers* Andrew O'Hagan

There is no summary, no A–Z listing of writers and their subjects. It is as difficult to summarise the effect our places have had on our writers as it is to record their voices and their ways of seeing.

But it's easy to summarise the effect their work has had on us. They've given the old place a coat of paint and kept the familiarities, so we know we belong. Scottish identity has been established and maintained by writers who imagined the ordinary, discovered the experienced and gave birth to an ancient, primitive place.

I had not believed that the stony heads
would change to actors and actresses,
and that the grooved armour of statues
would rise and walk away

into a resurrection of villages
townspeople, citizens, dead exiles.
who sing with the salt in their mouths,
winged nightingales of brine.

From *Listen* Iain Crichton Smith

A Man's a Man

We dare be poor . . .

From *A Man's a Man* Robert Burns

When Sheena Wellington sang *A Man's a Man* at the opening of the Scottish Parliament, it was a moment of restoration in more ways than one. For the first time in centuries, the Scottish people heard their language in an official setting.

The Parliamentary Union of 1707 completed a process that had begun with the Reformation, when English became the Word of God. It was now the language of government, officialdom, formality and gentility.

> What force or guile could not subdue
> Thro' many warlike ages
> Is wrought now by a coward few
> For hireling traitor's wages.
> The English steel we could disdain
> Secure in valour's station;
> But English gold has been our bane –
> Such a parcel of rogues in a nation!
> From *A Parcel of Rogues*
> *in a Nation* Robert Burns

In domestic politics, and notwithstanding a sentimental attachment to Jacobitism, Burns was a patriot who bitterly regretted the loss of Scottish independence. In *A Parcel of Rogues* he castigates the commissioners who negotiated the 1707 Act of Union that reduced the country to a 'region'.

Like MacDiarmid, his views in party political terms are contradictory. He clearly found inspiration in Bruce and Wallace, whose story, he told Dr John Moore, 'poured a Scottish prejudice into my veins which will boil along there until the floodgates of life shut in eternal rest'.

The basis of Burns' political beliefs can be found in his background and humanitarian nature, which stemmed from the sense of pride and self-respect many Scots feel is their birthright. This theme occurs time and again in his poems, songs and letters:

> It's no in titles nor in rank:
> It's no in wealth like Lon'on Bank,
>   To purchase peace and rest.
> It's no in makin muckle, mair;
> It's no in books; it's no in lear,   learning
>   To make us truly blest:
> If happiness hae not her seat
>   An' centre in the breast,
> We may be wise, or rich, or great,
>   But never can be blest!
> Nae treasures nor pleasures
>   Could make us happy lang;
> The heart ay's the part ay
>   That makes us right or wrang.
>   From *Epistle to Davie* Robert Burns

This dignity lies at the heart of his finest expression of universal brotherhood; and by stating the simple truth that 'a man's a man for a' that', Burns gave us a legacy greater than any other, a declaration of common humanity that has, in effect, been the conscience of our people.

Andrew O'Hagan sees the Burns' song as a precursor to a political feeling that is native to Scottish writing. 'It's a very indirect kind of politics,' he says. 'It's not about saying here's where to put your mark on the voting paper. It's about first principals, it's about metaphysics, it's about saying this is who we are, and this is how moral life begins.'

And William McIlvanney has no doubt about the song's importance. 'A Man's a Man is for me the most succinct, trenchant dismissal of titled status in the history of literature.'

The clarity of Burns' ideal has appealed to Scottish writers as strongly as it has appealed to the Scottish people and has been a rallying call for the standards of social justice to be manifest in Scottish society.

At the opening of the Parliament, Donald Dewar said, 'At the heart of that song is a very Scottish conviction: that honesty and simple dignity are priceless virtues, not imparted by rank or birth or privilege, but part of the soul.'

The song is a testament to the times in which it was written. Burns sent the song to George Thomson in January 1795, saying they were 'two or three pretty good prose thoughts, inverted into rhyme'.

Europe had been badly shaken by the French Revolution of 1789. In a letter to Mrs Frances Dunlop, written on 12 January 1795, Burns referred to the executions of Louis XVI and Marie Antoinette: 'What is there in the delivering of a perjured Blockhead and an unprincipled prostitute to the hands of the hangman, that it should arrest for a moment, attention, in an eventful hour, when as my friend Roscoe in Liverpool gloriously expresses it – when the welfare of millions is hung in the scale. And the balance yet trembles with fate.'

Mrs Dunlop's position – she was the eldest daughter of Sir Thomas Wallace of Craigie – meant she was aghast at Burns' letter. She ignored his subsequent correspondence, until Burns wrote to her on 10 July 1796, eleven days before his death. Her reply was one of the last things Burns read.

A new method of thinking had arisen. Thomas Paine's The Rights of Man took its inspiration from the French Revolution and advocated the overthrow of the British ruling establishment. The book sold 200,000 copies in Britain and became something of a bestseller in Scotland, especially after it had been translated into Gaelic. Burns' support for Tom Paine's ideas was tempered by his position as a tenant farmer and government employee, though it contained some observations he would have found familiar and appealing;

The aristocracy are not the farmers who work the land, and raise the produce, but are the mere consumers of the rent; and when compared with the active world are the drones . . . who neither collect the honey nor form the hive, but exist only for last enjoyment.

From The Rights of Man Thomas Paine

Burns had read *The Rights of Man* in the summer of 1792, when Thomas Muir of Huntershill and William Skirving founded the Scottish Friends of the People. On 22 September that year the National Convention declared France a republic; and the persecutions and repressions that followed the revolution were given fresh impetus. The Pitt government was nervous about developments in North Britain.

Captain William Johnston founded the *Edinburgh Gazetteer* in November 1792 and Burns become a subscriber, encouraging Johnston to, 'Lay bare, with undaunted heart & steady hand, that horrid mass of corruption called Politics & State-Craft!' Burns had met Johnston in Edinburgh and sent him two poems.

Writing to Mrs Dunlop on 6 December, Burns explained that in the Dumfries theatre, '"God Save the King" has met with some groans and hisses, while "Ça ira" [the French revolutionary song] has been repeatedly called for.'

And before the year was out an informer told the Excise Board that Burns was 'head of a disaffected party' in Dumfries. He was accused of being a Republican. The Collector of Excise was instructed to investigate.

The threat of economic and political repercussions caused Burns to write to Robert Graham of Fintry on Hogmanay, 1792. Robert Graham was a Commissioner of the Scottish Board of Excise who had helped Burns to secure his Excise post; the two had met on Burns' Highland tour in 1787.

Burns said the investigation had left him 'surprised, confounded and distracted . . . Sir, you are a Husband – and a father – you know what you would feel to see the much-loved wife of your bosom, and your helpless, prattling little ones, turned adrift into the world, degraded and disgraced from a situation in which they had been respectable and respected, and left almost without the necessary support of a miserable existence. – Alas, Sir! Must I think that such, soon, will be my lot! And from the damned, dark insinuations of hellish, groundless Envy too! . . . To the British Constitution . . . next to my God, I am most devoutly attached!'

And on 5 January 1793, he again wrote to Graham, answering what would appear to be specific charges. He had been in the playhouse when 'Ça ira' was called for, but did not join in the anthem; he will ever revere the Monarch of Great Britain. He cites his Masonic credentials. The British Constitution is, he says, the most glorious on earth. He knows nothing of Johnston and if Graham thinks he acted improperly he will withdraw the subscription to his paper. He was, at one time, an enthusiastic supporter of France but recent events made him 'alter my sentiments'.

The surprising thing is how Burns managed to maintain his position and still find ways of expressing his radical beliefs. He had told Mrs Dunlop on 6 December, he was 'a Placeman . . . so much so as to gag me from joining the cry. – What my private sentiments are, you will find out without an Interpreter.'

On 1 February 1793, the French Republic declared war on Britain and government suppression increased. Thomas Muir and the leaders of the Friends of the People were arrested. Among the charges laid at Muir's door was that he had passed *The Rights of Man* to his friends.

Muir's story is worthy of a Hollywood epic, though there seems to have been little or no romantic interest. In a letter dated 'About 30 August 1793', the date fixed for Muir's trial, Burns sent George Thomson the manuscript for *Scots Wha' Hae*. A postscript refers to 'that glorious struggle for Freedom, associated with the glowing ideas of some other struggles of the same nature, *not quite so ancient*.

If there had been doubt about the state's position, the appointment of Lord Braxfield revealed its intention. As Robert Macqueen he had acted for the Crown in cases concerning the forfeiture of estates following the 1745 Jacobite rebellion and was presiding judge at the trial of Deacon Brodie, Edinburgh's prototype master of dual identity, town councillor by day and burglar by night. Brodie was Stevenson's model for Dr Jekyll and Braxfield duplicated into *Weir of Hermiston*.

At a time when the features of the most powerful politician in Scotland, Henry Dundas, who instigated Muir's trial, were said to be 'tinged with a convivial purple' and when Dr Alexander Webster, minister of St Giles, was nicknamed Dr Bonum Magnum because he could drink five bottles of claret at a sitting and (reputedly) remain sober, the Scottish judiciary were certainly no sluggards when it came to boozing. Henry Cockburn immortalises some prodigious topers while praising the clarity of their judgements.

Braxfield presided with a bottle of claret to hand. He could make the indicted tremble in the dock, was described by a contemporary as 'a man without heart or pity' and told one accused, 'You're a very clever chiel, but you'd be nane the waur o' a hanging.'

The verdict at Muir's trial was a foregone conclusion. He was sentenced to fourteen years' transportation and his Friends of the People associates were similarly dismissed. Braxfield's hand-picked jurors were shocked at the severity of the sentences. Reform, they were told, was unconstitutional and only landed interests had a right to be represented in government. The issue was raised in Parliament, but the sentences stood. Dundas had fired a warning shot: this was the least a radical could expect.

In December 1794 Burns was promoted to Acting Supervisor of Excise and on 31 January 1795 became a founder member of the

Dumfries Volunteers. A few months later he wrote the emble-matically patriotic *Does Haughty Gaul Invasion Threat?* which was first published in the *Edinburgh Courant* in May 1795.

In January 1795 he'd sent *A Man's a Man* to George Thomson, editor of *Selected Scottish Airs*, published in June 1793, to which Burns had contributed twenty-five songs. He also sent his friend William Stewart at Closeburn Castle 'a painful, disagreeable letter; and the first of the kind I ever wrote'. He was in serious distress for three or four guineas.

As Burns suspected would happen, and the accompanying note suggests, Thomson was fearful of controversy and did not publish the song until 1805, after it had become popular. *A Man's a Man* first appeared anonymously in the *Glasgow Magazine* in August 1795, in *The Oracle* the following year, when it was issued as a chapbook in Paisley, and in August 1797 it was published in *The Scots Magazine*.

There can be little doubt that the government's spy network would have judged the song seditious. However, it was not until it was reprinted under Burns' name in the pro-government London-based *Oracle* that the authorities took notice. Burns died that year, aged thirty-seven.

The tune and some of the phrases were used in the first of four satirical election ballads written for his friend Patrick Heron, who stood as Whig candidate in the 1795 by-election for a Member of Parliament for the Stewartry of Kirkcudbright. The refrain 'for a' that and a' that' is repeated in the fifth line of each stanza and 'wi' ribbard star and a' that' is used in the fourth stanza, again to satirise the aristocracy.

That the song expresses Burns' opinions is beyond doubt. It acclaims his radicalism and generosity of spirit; something Scots feel is part of their national identity. It replicates and in many ways conveniently parcels the sober realities of the Scottish Enlight-enment. David Hume and others sought a benign society, a place where sense and worth would bear the gree, where human nature controlled destinies, where people were basically innocent and good; dignified because of who rather than what they were.

Who will not sing God save the King
Shall hang as high's the steeple;
But while we sing God save the King,
We'll ne'er forget the People!

From *Does Haughty Gaul*
Invasion Threat? Robert Burns

Another, less obvious, act of restoration that took place at the opening of our parliament was that the words were sung rather than recited. It used to be common to hear Burns' songs spoken, though the tunes were obviously familiar. Until recently, the songs were, and often still are, printed without the tunes, though the tune is almost always named.

It's easier to explain why this happened with the ballads. The early collectors were mostly poets who were more interested in the text than the tune. Until the folk song revival of the 1960s, ballads were generally recited or performed in art song arrangements that rarely suited the text. There was a received opinion about what constituted good singing. The standard was art song, whether it suited the material or not, and there are many examples of words and music becoming subservient to a singers' language or technique. It was common to hear songs written in Scots being sung in Anglified Scots, English or in a mid-Atlantic pop style. And no songwriter suffered more than Burns.

'There is an implicit assumption in much literary criticism that the music of Burns' songs is a minor factor which must be recognised by the critic but with reluctance,' writes Cedric Thorpe Davie in an essay on *Robert Burns, Writer of Songs.* 'In fact, the songs are the result of the fusion of two elements from different arts. In the best examples this fusion is complete, and the elements are inseparable without vital injury to one or both. But for the tunes, the words would never have come into existence, and it is absurd to regard the latter as poetry to be read or spoken aloud.'

One-fifth of Burns' songs, he says, are real successes, 'some of them outstandingly so, as integrated and unified products [which] puts him on a level with most great creative artists. Schubert in his 600 songs did not achieve such a proportion, and a disinterested assessment of the lyric output of any of the great poets or composers would usually lead to a similar conclusion.'

Burns has an ability to address the reader directly and make his work become part of the reader's experience. The appeal of his song lyrics, like the ballads, lies in their simplicity, which makes them wonderfully metrical, easily memorised and perfect for recitation. A Man's a Man is composed mainly of one- or two-syllable words, with a two- three- and a single four-syllable word; 'poverty' and 'dignities' occurring in the first and fourth verses; and 'independent' in verse three.

Burns' directness means he carries his readers with him. We believe what he says, even if he says something different, even diametrically opposite, elsewhere. We believe what he says because of his conviction. More than any other writer he convinces us he cannot pretend to feelings he does not possess. He may feel something different later, and his letters often suggest as much, but when we read him, we believe what he says.

Edwin Morgan's assertion that there is no one quite like him is something Scottish working people have felt instinctively for generations. Burns was my mother's favourite poet and the only poet I remember being quoted outside the classroom during the whole of my childhood. My mother's edition of Burns' poems was given to my father when he left for the Second World War. It was lost the first time his ship was torpedoed and his own edition was a gift from the Lord Provost and City of Glasgow, given to all servicemen at a concert in the St Andrew's Halls. Woody Guthrie and Cisco Houston were at the same concert.

An uncle of mine used to quote Burns on questions of morality and etiquette before the Bible, another knew more than 200 pieces by heart. The poet and playwright Janet Paisley's experience is not untypical: 'The first time I came across Robert Burns was when I was very young, possibly four or five. It was in my uncle's house. He took this book out of the cupboard and said, "Listen to this."

He didn't look at the pages and recited this poem to me which was *A Man's a Man for a' That*. At that age I was just completely baffled because of course a man was a man, what else could he be? A donkey? A dug? A cat? He wasnae, he was a man. And I couldn't understand why in reading it my uncle's eyes were full of tears.'

A Man's a Man is far from the only place where Burns expresses these ideals. *The Twa Dogs*, written in 1786, is crammed with telling details about the harsh, exposed and exhausting nature of farm work in the late eighteenth century, as opposed to the pampered sloth of the aristocracy:

> Lord Man our gentry care as little,
> For delvers, ditchers and sic cattle . . .

Scottish society had begun the painful transformation from a predominantly agrarian economy. The new, urban working class was concentrated around the ironworks, mines and shipyards. Burns made his views apparent in the few lines he wrote on a visit to the Carron Ironworks:

> We cam na here tae view your warks
> In hopes to be mair wise,
> But only, lest we gang to Hell,
> It may be nae surprise.

The social and economic transformation was unparalleled in its speed, scale and intensity. Between 1750 and 1850 the rate of town and city growth in Scotland was faster than any region in Britain or the Continent. Between 1780 and 1830 Glasgow's population rose to around 200,000. Massive immigration accompanied the shift of people from rural to urban environments. Impoverished Irish and Highland families arrived on every tide. Glasgow's population trebled between 1800 and 1830, yet the housing stock remained static.

I'll sing a song of Glasgow town
Where wealth and want abound;
Where the high seat of learning dwells
Mid ignorance profound.
Oh, when will Glasgow make a rule
To do just what she ought –
Let starving bairns in every school
Be fed as well as taught!
And when will Glasgow city be
Fair Caledonia's pride,
And boast her clear unclouded skies,
And crystal-flowing Clyde?

From *A Song of Glasgow Town* Marion Bernstein

And while society rejected Burns' universal vision, another Ayrshire writer recorded the transition. John Galt was born in Irvine in 1779. His family moved to Greenock ten years later and Galt completed his education at the local grammar school.

The route from Ayrshire to Greenock was well established and in 1795 the Greenock Ayrshire Society was founded to help immigrants. On 21 July 1801, the sixth anniversary of the poet's death, the Greenock Burns Club and Ayrshire Society was created from the Greenock Ayrshire Society. And on January 25 the following year, the world's first Burns Club held the first Burns Supper.

By this time John Galt was contributing essays, verse and stories to local publications and in 1804 he moved to London. In public John Galt was an eager young businessman hoping to make his fortune. As a parliamentary lobbyist Galt hung around the corridors of power, nursing bills through parliament, where he proudly claimed he had upwards of sixty acquaintances. In private John Galt was a solitary writer.

He tried to keep his careers separate, but they collided after he had spent two years travelling through Europe and the Near East, where he met and befriended Byron, eventually publishing a biography of the poet in 1830. On his return to London, he published an account of his travels, a life of Cardinal Wolsey and a collection of five short tragedies.

He contributed regularly to the *Monthly Magazine*, wrote a number of textbooks and in 1820 *Blackwood's Magazine* serialised and eventually published Galt's first novel *The Ayrshire Legatees*. Correspondence between Galt and William Blackwood suggests the publisher thought his work was suitable for a 'vulgar' class of reader. Galt complained; he couldn't understand why Blackwood should publish 'my things for a lower class of readers than those for whom the works of others are intended'.

The conflict came to a head with Galt's third novel *The Entail*, which Blackwood published in 1823. Galt complained he was 'over-persuaded' to alter the story and Blackwood's interference had hindered his progress.

Galt had written *Annals of the Parish* some eight or nine years before it was published in 1821: 'When my work was finished I wrote to my old acquaintance Constable, the bookseller, what I was about, but he gave me no encouragement to proceed: Scottish novels, he said, would not do.'

The unfinished manuscript was thrown into a drawer and forgotten. It was too local and too Scottish. In the meantime, Scott's success with *Waverley* had made Scottish novels popular. Galt dusted down *Annals* and fashioned them into shape. When Blackwood's serialisation of *The Ayrshire Legatees* proved popular he asked Galt for more. Galt sent *Annals of the Parish* and Blackwood published it immediately.

In an age of prolific writers, Galt was amazingly industrious. He had developed the habit of writing quickly in between his dubious business and political ventures. Between 1820 and 1823 he produced five novels.

In 1824 he became secretary to the Canada Company, a group set up to encourage emigration. Between 1825 and 1829 Galt visited Canada as part of a government commission and in 1826 founded the city of Guelph in Ontario.

In my works I have not attained excellence, but some of them are considered not without merit, and those have made their way to their little prominence, without the advocacy of any associate, or any effort on my own part, directly or indirectly, to make them known . . . Enough, however, of literature is before the public, by which my station as an author may be determined. But I shall not be justly dealt with if I am considered merely as a literary man: all that I have done ought to be taken into the estimate, and against many faults and blemishes many cares should be placed, disappointments, ill-requited struggles, and misfortunes of no common kind, with the depressing feeling, in calamitous circumstances, of how much I stood in the need of heartening from a friend.

But when my numerous books are forgotten, I shall yet be remembered. At a period when all the assurance of a provision for my family was announced to be a fallacy, I contrived the Canada Company, which will hereafter be spoken of among the eras of a nation destined to greatness. That project, flourishingly carried into effect, I not only projected, but established myself; and lands, now more extensive than all the arable land in Scotland are in process of settlement, and attractive to the super abundant population of the United Kingdom.

From *The Literary Life & Miscellanies* John Galt

Galt returned to Britain in 1829 with massive debts and spent several months in a debtors' prison. He settled in Greenock, where he wrote a number of novels, an autobiography and autobiographical sketches.

In *Annals of the Parish*, Galt was the first writer to show the effects the burgeoning Industrial Revolution was having on the people of Scotland. Novels such as *Annals of the Parish* and *The Ayrshire Legatees* made him the first political novelist in the English language.

His reputation has been overshadowed firstly by Scott and secondly by Hogg but he is now being recognised as one of the great writers of the age, whose best work, mostly written at speed in three years, represents what the textbook *Scottish Literature* calls 'one of the truly great publishing records of any Scottish novelist'.

Andrew O'Hagan is a Galt admirer. 'One of the great things that can happen in a literature is that things can get buried for a few years. They can slightly disappear from view, and then re-emerge; and somebody who's always re-emerging, but never taking centre stage, is John Galt; in the 1830s, I think, the best writer in Scotland.'

Annals of the Parish observes how a small rural community develops into a complex town. The story covers half a century and the action is seen through the eyes of Micah Balwhidder, a Presbyterian minister, for whom his parish is the world in microcosm. 'What happened in my parish was but a type and index to the rest of the world,' he says.

Novelist Chris Dolan points out, 'Galt does what Burns does, something very innovative; he writes about very ordinary people in very ordinary situations. Burns had just a little touch of what would become the Kailyard, just a little touch of romanticism, painting in brighter and prettier colours. But Galt was more in tune with what would happen in Russia later, to the point where *Annals of the Parish* was thought for many years to be a diary rather than a novel.'

And the poet Tracey Herd finds the structure adds to the illusion. 'The book is a mixture of the homely and the grand. Micah Balwhidder mixes his own experience with what is happening in the village and by extension in the world outside, so that there's this constant interplay between the personal and the general, something that is very unusual in Scottish fiction and for the time absolutely remarkable.'

All the boys of Garnock assembled at the Braehead. The wives with their sucklings were seated on the large stones at

their respective door cheeks. Their lassie weans, like cluster-
ing bees were mounted on the carts. The old men took their
stations on the dyke that encloses the side of the vinter's
kailyard; and a batch of wabster lads with green aprons and
then, yellow faces, planted themselves at the gable of the
malt-kin.

From Annals of the Parish John Galt

And the arrival of a newspaper was an epic moment.

But, in the midst of all this commercing and manufacturing,
I began to discover signs of decay in the wonted simplicity of
our country ways. Among the cotton-spinners and muslin-
weavers of Cayenneville, were several unsatisfied and ambitious spirits, who clubbed together and got a London newspaper to the Cross Keys, where they were nightly in the habit
of meeting and debating about the affairs of the French,
which were then gathering toward a head.

From Annals of the Parish John Galt

Andrew O'Hagan comments on Galt's story *The Seamstress*. 'The
central character is just a woman sewing and he uses a very
Scottish word to describe her carefulness, *eident*, she's there with
eident care sewing this piece of fabric. Then you suddenly realise,
this is 1831, Galt is bringing into Scottish literature the notion of
the worker, of the smaller person, of the ordinary individual.'

Galt's work was condemned. The unmarried pregnancies and
raciness were unacceptable in an age of cultivation and refinement.
Susan Ferrier described him as 'unspeakably vulgar', saying Galt's
novel *Sir Andrew Wylie* 'beats print'.

But she and other critics were missing the point. For the first
time in literature Galt suggested that the coming of industrialisation pitted man's faith in himself against his faith in God. And he
goes some way to making Burns' sentiment visible. He strikes a
blow for democracy, while illustrating that neither aristocracy nor

the church can pretend social change isn't happening. And change is happening quickly, in the span of one parish minister's tenancy.

And call they this Improvement? – to have changed,
My native Clyde, my once romantic shore,
Where Nature's face is banish'd and estranged,
And heaven reflected in thy wave no more;
Whose banks, that sweeten'd May-day's breath before,
Lie sere and leafless now in summer's beam,
With sooty exhalations cover'd o'er;
And for the daisied green-sward, down thy stream
Unsightly brick-lanes smoke, and clanking engines gleam.

From *Lines on Revisiting*
a Scottish River Thomas Campbell

Within seven years of Scott's death in 1832, we had lost a remarkable generation of writers. Hogg died in 1835 and Galt was buried in Greenock four years later. Their impact is still felt today, which led to the belief that Scottish writing then went into decline. That's now seen as something of a fiction, though we certainly lacked writers of such striking originality and depth.

Apart from Thomas Carlyle and Hugh Miller, we lacked writers who could explain what was happening, socially and politically, who could challenge the dominant voices of the time, and, rather than highlight aspects of industrialisation, show, or even indicate, the entirety of its impact.

The Burns' ideal was an inspiration and many writers carried his inherent political message to a logical conclusion; though, to a large extent, our talent for discourse took over. George MacDonald's novels later inspired J.R.R. Tolkien and C.S. Lewis, who called him 'My master; indeed I fancy I have never written a book in which I did not quote from him.' Margaret Oliphant shared MacDonald's hatred of industrialisation, while poets such as James Young Geddes and John Davidson continued the tradition of inclusiveness. T.S. Eliot and Hugh MacDiarmid acknowledged their debts to Davidson, especially for the ways he explored influences beyond the Scots tradition.

James Thomson replicated the twins of urban despair and materialism in *City of Dreadful Night*, portraying London as a wasteland, as well as making a powerful statement of Victorian loss of faith; and, as Tom Leonard's anthology *Radical Renfrew* shows, many writers whose names are not immediately familiar were prepared to address the social issues of the time.

There were individual voices, but nothing of the force we'd known, and it took a new century for an assessment of the hatred and exploitation that for many typified the rise of industrialisation to arrive from an unlikely source.

George Douglas Brown's *The House with the Green Shutters* was published in 1901. It traces the fall of John Gourlay, a self-made man with great ambitions, and it was specifically written as a reaction to the most popular fiction of the time, the Kailyard, using the ingredients of its novels to impart the antithesis of couthie, idealised, small town domesticity.

Brown grew up in the pretty Ayrshire village of Ochiltree, an area Burns knew well. He was the illegitimate son of the master of nearby Drumsmudden Farm and one of his dairymaids, and endured the daily taunt, 'There goes Smudden's bastard!'

Brown admired John Galt and *The House with the Green Shutters* tries to recreate accurately Scottish speech and small town life. At the heart of the novel is a conflict which reflects Stevenson and anticipates Grassic Gibbon. The book depicts the village of Barbie in the throes of social and economic transition, and explores a number of sensitive autobiographical themes. It is without doubt one of the most important books in Scottish literary history.

Brown took the elements which comprise a kailyard novel and injected them with a lethal dose of realism. Kailyard novels reinforced the model of rural idealism. No matter what happened to the characters, all would be well in the end and they would learn some pointed moral lesson.

The character of Gourlay is memorable because of his capacity for hatred. The novel is set in the type of idyllic, rural landscape that previously suggested communitarianism in Burns: a place where natural harmony reigns. 'And here's Gourlay with his harmony,' says Andrew O'Hagan. 'He'll have none of it. There's a sense that he represents a very brutal streak in the Scottish male psyche.'

Gourlay's business is ruined. His weak, drink-sodden son fails at university. His consumptive daughter and sluttish wife commit suicide after a final majestic reading of St Paul's letter to the Corinthians on the theme of charity. His son murders Gourlay, then commits suicide. Gourlay represents obsession and domination, and shows what can happen when such a person becomes separated from any sense of community.

Chris Dolan finds the sheer acidity of the novel and the vigour of the language overwhelming: 'I can't believe that a man could hate so much. He hates everybody. Every single character is drawn with the most precise lines, like a knife edge cutting through them all.'

And while Tracey Herd agrees, she finds a sense of repression in Gourlay, which carries a contemporary resonance. 'It's not that he's beyond the finer feelings. His hatred is overwhelming, but it's as if he sees humans as something less than the animal, as if the human condition is bound to fail him, while the simple devotion of an animal provides him with an emotional dimension. We see him weeping when his horse dies, but at no other time.'

Hate was the greater on both sides because it was often impotent. Gourlay frequently suspected offence and seethed because he had no idea how to meet it – except by driving slowly down the brae in his new gig and never letting on when the Provost called to him. That was a wipe in the eye for the Provost! The 'bodies', on their part, could rarely get near enough Gourlay to pierce his armour; he kept them off him by his brutal dourness. For it was not only pride and arrogance, but a consciousness, also, that he was no match for them at their own game, that kept Gourlay away from their society.

From *The House with the Green Shutters* George Douglas Brown

The 'bodies' are the people of Barbie, the ordinary folk that Gourlay despises. Douglas Brown uses them as a Greek chorus, commenting on and anticipating the tragedy.

John stood there, suddenly weak in his limbs, and stared, as if petrified, at the red poker in his hand. A little wisp of grizzled hair stuck to the square of it, severed, as by scissors, between the sharp edge and the bone. It was the sight of that bit of hair that roused him from his stupor – it seemed so monstrous and horrible, sticking all by itself to the poker. 'I didna strike him so hard.'

From *The House with the Green Shutters* George Douglas Brown

Andrew O'Hagan is in no doubt about the novel's importance. 'In every generation,' he says, 'a novel comes along which sometimes by accident, sometimes purely by design, unseats all the previous slack thinking in the culture, and *The House with the Green Shutters* was a novel like that.'

It provided a counterpoint to the Utopian vision of *A Man's a Man* by highlighting how commerce and industry were tearing at the fabric of Scottish society; and in so doing provided the matrix for a new century of Scottish literature.

The dominant voice of the new century belonged to Christopher Murray Grieve. Writing under the pseudonym of Hugh MacDiarmid he hammered his way into the Scottish consciousness, urging a process of re-education of the Scottish public. He founded what he called the Scottish Renaissance Movement, and through a series of newspaper articles, essays, books, reviews, poems, speeches, stories, at least one playscript and a lost, unfinished novel he urged us to look outwards, to find new ways of thinking, to find intellectual trail-blazers rather than heroes. He despised mediocrity and was especially critical of the Burns cult, which he felt demeaned the poet and his achievements.

He urged us to go back to William Dunbar, whose work, he said, provided an antidote to what he saw as the mire Scottish writing had descended into in the post-Burns age:

No' wan in fifty kens a wurd Burns wrote
But misapplied is a'body's property,
And gin there was his like alive the day
They'd be the last a kennin' haund to gi'e . . .
As Kirks wi' Christianity hae dune,
Burns Clubs wi' Burns – wi' a' thing it's the same,
The core o' ocht is only for the few,
Scorned by the mony, thrang wi'ts empty name.

From *A Drunk Man Looks at the Thistle* Hugh MacDiarmid

Only a cultural renaissance could create a climate of creativity that would restore our sense of worth, individually and nationally. His disputes almost always became personal, and while the roles of writer and propagandist mingled easily, his opinions were rarely difficult to understand. MacDiarmid's position was leftist, though he was also a nationalist whose perspective went far beyond any party political programme:

I am horrified by the triviality of life, by its corruptions and
  helplessness,
No prospect of eternal life, no fullness of existence, no love
  without betrayal,
No passion without satiety. Yet life could be beautiful even
  now.
But all is soiled under philistine rule. What untouched
  spiritual powers

Are hidden in the dark and cold, under the suffocating
atmosphere
Of philistine life, waiting for a better time when the first ray
of light
And breath of fresh air will call them to life and let them
unfold?

From Lament for the Great Music Hugh MacDiarmid

Like the earlier writers, his radicalism was expansive and his
polemics direct. He saw political advancement as the first step
towards a better use of our physical and spiritual resources, an idea
he expressed in *A Drunk Man Looks at the Thistle* and which he
returned to in later work, and something which made him admire
the concentration of Lenin's vision.

His one-man renaissance attracted poets who wrote outstand-
ing work in Scots, poets such as William Soutar, Sydney Goodsir
Smith and Robert Garioch, yet MacDiarmid's work is in danger of
being drowned in the swell of his many contradictions and
personality, especially the ways in which the national inferiority
complex became incorporated into his work and opinions. He is
liable to be viewed as a cultural bombast rather than as a writer. It's
a judgement he would have hated.

One of the many things he achieved by demanding a review of
Dunbar was to instigate a reassessment of Burns' work, to see it in
the light of its creation, as the poet saw it. And no writer
embraces the spirit of the Burns' song more closely than Mac-
Diarmid:

There is no great problem in the world today
Except disease and death men cannot end
If no man tries to dominate another.
The struggle for material existence is over. It has been won.
The need for repressions and disciplines has passed.
The struggle for truth and that indescribable necessity,
Beauty, begins now, hampered by none of the lower needs.

No one now needs live less or be less than his utmost . . .
. . . It is now the duty of the Scottish genius
Which has provided the economic freedom for it
To lead in the abandonment of creeds and moral
    compromises
Of every sort and to commence to express the unity of life.
From *Lament for the Great Music* Hugh MacDiarmid

It would be narrow-minded to see the Scottish Renaissance in terms of writers who were influenced by or associated with MacDiarmid alone. From the 1930s onward there was no shortage of writers anxious to reflect the dominant political issues of the time. The most realistic and clearest political statement is Lewis Grassic Gibbon's *A Scots Quair*, but Neil Gunn, Edwin Muir, Eric Linklater and James Barke also widened the range and direction.

George Blake was convinced that what became known as the urban kailyard deflected attention from the urban working class, and he tried to address this in *The Shipbuilders*, published in 1935. It's an epic story, describing two people, one at the bow and the other at the stern of the class struggle; a shipyard owner and the riveter who had been his wartime batman. Now regarded as an important attempt at a proletarian novel, with some fine writing in places, at the time it was heavily criticised, especially for its unrealistic dialogue. Blake admitted he was 'guilty of an insufficient knowledge of working-class life and to the adoption of a middle-class attitude to the theme of industrial conflict and despair'.

While some were failing nobly, and others were attempting to over-sentimentalise working-class life, another school of writers was emerging in the form of the over-dramatic 'Hard Man'. A stereotype was born.

No Mean City was also published in 1935, *The New York Herald Tribune* proclaiming that it 'reeks with squalor and ends in triumph'. They called it 'an astonishing, important and inspiring book'. Glasgow City Libraries refused to stock it, but seventy years later, it remains the best known Glasgow novel, at least by name.

The range and diversity of Scottish writing in the 1930s is by any standards remarkable. Eric Linklater's elegant and stylish comedies contrasted with A.J. Cronin's recreation of themes from *The House with the Green Shutters* in novels like *Hatter's Castle* and *The Citadel*; Neil Gunn and Naomi Mitchison worked with history and mysticism; Catherine Carswell, Dot Allen, Nan Shepherd and Nancy Brysson Morrison sought to offer a new and affirmative approach to the role of women in contemporary society.

In *Scottish Scene*, Gibbon and MacDiarmid provided a list of contemporary writers, adding that 'Scotland never at any previous time possessed so numerous a corps of novelists; that the general level of its novelistic ability was never higher; and that the "native content" of its novels was never keener or greater.'

In a number of novels, the social awareness and characterisation were powerful elements, although they adopted Blake's stance of looking in from outside. In 1939 James Barke published *The Land of the Leal*, which depicted a peasant family's journey from Galloway to Glasgow, finishing during the Depression. His heroine Jean Ramsay mirrored Chris Guthrie's indomitability. And in the same year Edward Gaitens published *The Sailing Ship*, a miracle of a short story, which later appeared in *Growing Up and Other Stories*. With Edward Gaitens, Scottish working-class literature found its true voice.

Gaitens' work has had a profound effect on Glasgow writers in particular and Scottish writing in general, though this influence may not be obvious. William McIlvanney only recently read Gaitens, yet Gaitens' honesty, his insight into youth and sensitivity, surely finds expression in McIlvanney's work, especially in a novel like *Docherty*. Both writers celebrate humanity, insist on the power of love, present a realistic picture of working-class family life and affirm the role of the community. These qualities are also reflected in Archie Hind's *The Dear Green Place*, as well as in the works of George Friel and Robin Jenkins.

In *The Sailing Ship* Johnny Regan is a brutalised and energetic working-class lad whose capacity for dreaming does not detach him from his surroundings. Despite an upbringing in the slums, Regan aspires to be a poet or a philosopher. His socialist beliefs and refusal to fight in the First World War lead him to be imprisoned as a conscientious objector. Johnny Regan's experience mirrors that of Gaitens who spent two years in prison during the First World War.

Johnny Regan is searching for an identity in a society where men are defined by their job, their war service or both. He is marooned in a time when work is difficult to come by and memories of the war are being wished away, or have become an excuse for bitterness. Regan's mother resents his survival when her favourite son fell.

Regan reappears in other guises in post-World War I novels. His desire for self-improvement does not embrace middle-class values. He wants a better life for the working class. It has little or nothing to do with economic improvement for him alone.

> From every by-street the sound of the hordes of tenement children, on holiday these times, came to him; laughing and calling, each day they marvellously discovered happiness, like some lovely jewel, in the gutters and back courts of the big city. His soul joined with them as they sported and ran, and he was lightened with belief that war and poverty would sometime vanish away like an evil dream and that wakened Man would stand amazed at his blundering and turn to find happiness as simply and innocently as those ragged children were finding it now.
>
> From *The Sailing Ship* Edward Gaitens

Gaitens' stories often find young men at a moment of discovery or resolve, revealing how they reach that position rather than what will happen. They are often imprisoned by their surroundings, brutalised and neglected, yet he turns these people into the perfect vehicles to express Burns' ideals by imbuing them with honesty and hope. They believe in a better life because of their experience. It is thoroughly reasonable, practical and far more than an intellectual ideal.

Critics compared Gaitens to Maxim Gorky and Sean O'Casey. Edwin Muir called *Growing Up* 'the most remarkable first book produced by any Scottish writer for several years' and H.G. Wells declared, 'I do not exaggerate when I say that at least two of these stories are among the most beautiful in the English language.'

Gaitens' only novel, *Dance of the Apprentices* is a compound of six stories from *Growing Up* with additional chapters.

The peace of poetry filled him up again, quelling antagonism, and a great pity for his parents welled up. He exonerated both of them. They were victims of 'The System'. Capitalism created poverty. Poverty made brutes and wastrels of human beings. Socialism would bring plenty and freedom for mankind. The pamphlets his friend had given him proved it so clearly. With useful enthusiasm he foresaw the end of social inequalities. There would be a 'Glorious Revolution'. All over the world 'wage slaves would cast off their chains'. He saw the 'New Order' at work. Men and women, magically altered, living like clear-eyed happy beings in whom love and courtesy never died.

From *Dance of the Apprentices* Edward Gaitens

In the factories, the workers felt alienated and detached from society. Their world had become faceless. People were beginning to lose a sense of who they were and needed to latch on to something. Eddy Macdonnel finds a sense of worth in a fusion of Burns and socialism.

Eddy's feelings were like a desire to embrace the world . . . he believed men would one day march in friendship 'Sunwards' – with every Capitalist converted to sharing 'The Fruits of the

Earth' which provided 'Plenty for All' – to end the fester of the slums and the beastliness of war. 'Rabbie Burns is right!' he thought, 'It's comin' yet for a' that! Man tae man the warld ower shall brithers be an' a' that!' He would have to be more courageous, more wholehearted from now on.

From *Dance of the Apprentices* Edward Gaitens

But by the end of the novel, the apprentices' hopes have not materialised. After the war, poets did what their predecessors had done after the Union of 1707, they looked to the country's traditional music and song, while critics wondered if Scottish writers could deal effectively with the issue of class.

As the streets where Gaitens set his stories were swept away and their communities sought a brighter life in Utopian housing schemes, writers like Robin Jenkins, Archie Hind and George Friel began to explore both the individual and the changing nature of Scottish society. During the 1960s and 1970s the novels of the 1930s were mostly out of print. Only the overtly middle-class novels survived. Robin Jenkins had been using working-class backgrounds since the 1950s but William McIlvanney was perceived as a new voice. After publishing three novels he turned to crime fiction, in the hope of connecting with the working class. He recognised the paradox that his third novel, *Docherty*, published in 1975 'was written for people most of whom would never read it'.

William McIlvanney was motivated to write because of 'the absence of the life I came from in what was called literature'. He wanted to 'write a book that would create a kind of literary genealogy for the people I came from'.

He explains: 'I think you don't really understand a place till it's imaginatively inhabited through literature and I suppose I wanted to do that with working-class life in Scotland. I think *Docherty* is about a man who believes in the values of working-class life. What struck me when I wrote the book is that a lot of literature of working-class life, like *Sons and Lovers*, was about the escapee, the guy who got away, and therefore it's a distorted view, he's always looking back; and I thought in many ways, impressive book though it is, *Sons and Lovers* was a kind of libel on working-class life because the artistic pretensions were celebrated.'

'Ah'll tell ye the sense,' Tam said. 'We walk a nerra line. Ah ken hoo nerra it is. Ah've walked it a'ma days. Us an' folk like us hiv goat the nearest thing tae nothin' in this world. A' that filters doon tae us is shite. We leeve in the sewers o' ither bastards' comfort. The only thing we've goat is wan anither. That's why ye never sell yer mates. Because there's nothin' left tae buy wi' whit ye get. That's why ye respect yer weemenkind. Because whit we make oorselves is whit we are. Because if ye don't, ye're provin' their case. Because the bastards don't believe we're folk! They think we're some-thin'. . . . less than that.'

From *Docherty* William McIlvanney

Set in the fictional mining town of Graithnock and based on McIlvanney's hometown of Kilmarnock, the novel tells the story of a tough and uncompromising father Tam Docherty and his son Conn. Tam struggles through the present while dreaming of and fighting for a better future.

'I suppose what I felt was missing was the voice,' says McIl-vanney, 'and the experience of the people I came from. If literature's anything, presumably it's a body of evidence testifying to what it was like to be alive at that time, and for me it was a body of evidence in which about 98% of the witnesses weren't called.'

The novelist Des Dillon's response was immediate, fulfilling McIlvanney's ambition. When he read *Docherty* he recognised the language he spoke, the language that was part of his community reproduced on the page.

'It was so powerful to me,' Dillon says. 'It was emotional. I started to feel worthwhile. Our culture had been shoved to the side for so long, but I found it finally being accepted in literature and felt as if I was a human being because my background was being accepted.'

But for McIlvanney, there's a moral dimension. 'Working-class people were always moral, because they lived in such hard circumstances. As Docherty says, we can't afford to mess about, to blur the lines. You live with strict scruples, or you fall apart, and I think it's easy to forget how crucial the maintenance of those values was; as Docherty says, This is all we have; blow this and there's nothing left.'

Scotland in the 1980s witnessed the disintegration of the same working communities that had been forged in the Industrial Revolution. The departure exacted a heavy price. Idealism of more than one colour was in short supply. And with the destruction of the communities the values that sustained them were also weakened.

Andrew O'Hagan is being deliberately provocative when he says the great muse of Scottish writing was Margaret Thatcher: 'If a muse can be understood to be somebody who drives people to such a pitch of anger, and of feeling disenfranchised that a literature grows out of it, then she was indeed the muse of Scottish literature.'

'What happens in the 1980s,' says novelist and short story writer, Ali Smith, 'with the changes of government as well is the sense of being marginalised, there is a really strong aesthetic seminal reaction; so what you get is a yelling of all the different voices at once. Suddenly everybody is yelling to be heard.'

Edwin Morgan and Iain Crichton Smith, with Liz Lochhead, Tom Leonard and Alasdair Gray, reflected the Burns ideal and the changes in society, which were more than a shift in landscape or one section imposing its will upon another through economic necessity. Class values were being questioned, while working communities came under attack. There was a shift in language and emphasis. Banks urged people to borrow rather than save. Unemployment became leisure. And everyone was urged to embrace capitalism.

She walks through the village
carrying her messages from the Co-op;
the mice are burrowing through the walls,
the rats gnaw at the potatoes

which her heart-stricken husband has gathered
in the haze of autumn,
sweat in beads on his forehead
black dirt on his hands.

Prices are going up
year after year,
soon even the harmless daffodil
will be valued in gold.
From *Crofter's Wife* Iain Crichton Smith

With the traditional values and certainties of working communities redundant, writers like James Kelman and later Irvine Welsh
identified a new underclass of people who had become marginalised to the point of invisibility. This new theme explored an
individual isolation where politics is the protagonist and, by
definition, cannot provide the answer. People are no longer
defined by their job or community. The sense of belonging and
expectation has gone; the hope that politics provided has been
replaced by alienation and for many the very idea of political
involvement is irrelevant.

Irvine Welsh's characters are addicts who have removed themselves from any form of community. They are even apart from
each other. Friendship is on the basis of need; their dreams are
drug-induced, their realities are grim; their recoveries are tem-
porary; and their end is imminent. For them, there is no such
thing as society, though someone has to pay. The society they
recognise owes them a living. Either way, they do not care.

In James Kelman's Booker Prize-winning novel, *How late it was,
how late*, the protagonist, Joe Samuels, known as Sammy, describes

himself as an 'alky boozebag bastard'. He is an ex-convict, pushing forty and back in Scotland, trying to make some sort of life for himself. He might go back to England where there could be a job, but he could get by with a bit of shoplifting and is living with Helen, whom we never meet. She's constantly out the house, probably because of his drinking. He remembers a row, but she's disappeared.

Sammy goes on benders. He awakens in a lane on a Sunday morning, suddenly blind after a two-day session. There was a fight and the police were called. They know his record and were none too pleased to see him. Sammy can't remember what happened and even if he could he wouldn't help the police. Helen's his immediate concern. He doesn't know where she is, needs her help and can't get his bearings.

Sammy has always been out of his depth. He is frustrated and bored, angry and bewildered. He is also kind and naïve, refuses to give up, and struggles against officialdom in the form of police, doctors and DSS inspectors. The implication, even from the friends who have abandoned him, is that he's feigning his blindness, that he's out to milk the system.

This process is continually debilitating, is designed to wear people down; but to Sammy it's nothing unusual, it's what's to be expected. And as the relentless isolation increases, Sammy's stature rises: Ye've got to batter on, know what I'm saying, ye've got to batter on, he tells his son at the end of the book.

He is enthused with courage and humanity and, because we have witnessed his internal life, been party to his thoughts and emotions, we think more of Sammy than he thinks of himself, understand his position and empathise with his plight.

Ye wake in a corner and stay there hoping yer body will disappear, the thoughts smothering ye; these thoughts; but ye want to remember and face up to things, just something keeps ye from doing it, why can ye no do it; the words filling yer head: then the other words; there's something wrong;

there's something far far wrong; ye're no a good man, ye're just no a good man. Edging back into awareness, of where ye are; here slumped in this corner, with these thoughts filling ye. And oh christ his back was sore; stiff, and the head pounding. He shivered and hunched up his shoulders, shut his eyes, rubbed into the corners with his fingertips; seeing all kinds of spots and lights. Where in the name of fuck . . .

From *How late it was, how late* James Kelman

Chris Dolan sees the camera closing in: 'Burns pans across Scotland and picks out the ordinary working man and the agricultural labourer. It gets closer and closer, moving into the industrial society, where we're looking into people's kitchens. By the time you get to Kelman he's looking into one person's mind, and a mind from which that person can't escape, and a reality, a political reality, a psychological reality, a reality from which there is no escape.'

And Des Dillon senses a parallel: 'I write to entertain people. I write because I like to tell stories. Jim's a great writer, but I believe he writes from an absolute political anchor. And it's the same sentiment as Burns in the sense that he says, Don't you judge me because I swear, don't judge me because I speak like this, don't judge, don't judge, don't judge. Don't be elitist.'

Kelman's characters are often alienated from themselves as well as from their environment. He catches them at a time when crisis threatens and resolution seems necessary, when their powerlessness is overwhelming and they are at their most vulnerable. His story *Not not while the giro* shows someone waiting for their life to begin, a character with the capacity for fantasising his existence, using his dreaming as a form of escape:

My lot is severely trying. For an approximate age I have been receiving money from the state. I am obliged to cease this malingering and earn an honest penny. Having lived in this fashion for so long I am well nigh unemployable and if I were an Industrial Magnate or a Captain of Industry I would certainly entertain doubts as to my capacity for toil. I am an idle goodfornothing. A neerdowell. The workhouse is too good for the likes of me. I own up. I am incompatible with this Great British Society.

From *Not not while the giro* James Kelman

This situation is developed in *The Busconductor Hines*, where Hines' life is 'a perplexing kettle of coconuts' and plans of emigrating to Australia are an idle dream. In *How late it was, how late* the realities of this existence are all too clear. Constantly, readers are forced to ask how they would react in a similar position. Kelman challenges his readers. He doesn't want sympathy or even understanding. He simply asks how we would cope in a similar position. There is still a sense of personal survival, but survival is harder, and a man's a man for a' that.

While McIlvanney celebrates the values of working-class communities, to Kelman such values are redundant. What he shares with McIlvanney is the attention he pays to folk who would otherwise be ignored, the dignity he bestows on his characters that gives their life meaning. He challenges the reader to do more than understand or sympathise. He challenges the reader to identify.

When *How late it was, how late* won the Booker Prize, a judge asked for the rules to be changed so that nothing like it could appear again. In Scotland, an indication of Kelman's status comes from the many ways in which he has been emulated. Writers like Janice Galloway, Duncan McLean and Irvine Welsh clearly shared Kelman's sympathies, were initially enthused by his style and have used his influence to find voices of their own.

And while there are those who believe contemporary Scottish writing presents a one-dimensional view of society, the fact remains that the range of Scotland's voices has never been so varied or so strong. The orthodoxies of sexual behaviour and repression are challenged as frequently as issues of language, class and political status are confronted. Our long tradition of poets who defy categorisation is being well maintained and though the tangled boundaries that have defined Scottish writing are still around, there has never been such a variety of voices heading off in different directions, using more than one language and forcing recognition on an international stage.

The appeal of the Burns' superlative lies in its inclusion; and the tradition of Scottish writing which carries the values of what used to be known as the professional and commercial classes is as much a part of Burns' egalitarianism as that of an 'alky boozebag bastard'.

As he sat looking at David he doubted if he had done the right thing. Would it have been better had the boy been brought up in the country? He had been delicate and their aunt had spoilt him. And now that he was twenty-three he was all too well acquainted with the town's ways.

David was slack.

Arthur had him in the business now and was trying to knock some kind of discipline into him, but it was uphill work. He might have done better to leave him to his father and his step-mother.

Why had they taken such a hate to this Highland woman that their father had married? After eleven years they still knew nothing against her, except that she had been a hired servant and was almost illiterate. Mungo, the only one who really knew her, had liked her well enough. Had they been unfair in keeping away so much from the old man? They had felt it, perhaps, a desecration of their mother's memory. But had that been reasonable? And now, they hardly knew their little half-sister Phoebe. Bel had asked what was to become of her. She had even suggested she should be brought to live at Ure Place. He wondered if he ought to let her come. His habit of taking responsibility for everybody told him he should. Bel had maintained that the child could not stay on at the farm with only Mungo and a household of crude farm-women.

From *Wax Fruit* Guy McCrone

When Guy McCrone's trilogy *Wax Fruit* was published in 1947 it sold more than a million copies worldwide. It was perfect post-war reading, returning as to a world of safer values and domestic tensions.

He follows the Moorhouse family from Victorian beginnings through industry and empire. The middle-class minutiae of family, social ambition, standing in the community and Christian values are the backbone of the book, where men attend to business and the women look after everything else.

McCrone has John Galt's detachment and eye for domestic detail, though his tone is nostalgic. He offers an older, more certain Glasgow where the middle classes are comfortable to the point of complacency. There are tinges of bitterness and some of the portraits are sharply drawn, but the characters show no concern for anything other than their own plight and never quite lose the obsessions and fears of the *nouveau riche*, a social group who, in the main, have elicited little response from Scottish writers.

McCrone rarely shows much more than the family and shies away from entering into the wider world. Nor does he raise a teacup towards social comment, as Douglas Brown did, though he often shares a similar tone. The book is a hymn to order and priorities. Politics are taken for granted.

This may seem removed from the Burns ideal but the very insularity is a warning against that which is familiar and safe. And the very act of protection prevents others from drawing near.

The constant tension between outward appearance and internal reality is at the heart of Ronald Frame's fiction. Though he was born and brought up in Glasgow, his stories, novels and novellas have international locations. He lived for a while in England, a place he says he found exotic, but which he always viewed with a stranger's eye.

His is the world of the upper middle classes, a world of nuances, secrets, intrigues and betrayals, a world of intolerant and snobbish communities, a world where pith o' sense and pride o' worth do not exist.

Frame's characters seem bound by convention, by a proper means of behaviour. They are lonely and live in a world of unspoken rules. Appearance is as important as Substance. There are certain things one does not discuss and for many an emotional life is a strange and dangerous territority.

Miss Caldwell and Miss McLeod had met in the late 'sixties, as recently retired ladies and as habituees of Miss Barclay's tea-room in Byres Road. Before their introduction they'd each had a partner to have coffee with, until at about the same time of one never-to-be-forgotten year they'd been abandoned – Miss Caldwell's fellow-buyer (from Wylie and Lochhead) had inexplicably been wooed by an elderly manufacturer of ball-bearings and married him and gone to live in a nice trim seaside bungalow in Largs; Miss McLeod's friend, who'd been a teacher like her (at the Academy), had returned at sixty-four years old to her calf country in the windy Mearns – leaving the two Misses, Caldwell and McLeod, seated high-and-dry at adjoining tables and with no one in that roomful of spinsters to speak to.

From *Paris* Ronald Frame

The Misses Caldwell and McLeod are vestiges of a way of life that has almost vanished. They epitomise the effects of social control, the way a moral code does not need to be stated to be effective. The gentility is ultimately destructive, guaranteeing distance and drawing them into a web of missed opportunities.

Frame's best book, *The Lantern Bearers*, is set in 1960s' Scotland.

The story is told by a lonely boy Neil Pritchard who is sent to the Solway Coast to live with an aunt while his parents separate.

The novel takes its title from a Robert Louis Stevenson essay in which children cover lanterns with their coats. They hide their light. It is a novel of discoveries, sexual, social and especially of the ways art in general and music in particular can dignify life in the midst of any crisis or personal tragedy. The warmth and honesty in Frame's book, the way Neil reaches out to be recognised, fulfil all Burns' criteria.

Allan Massie is among the finest Scottish writers of his generation. His international reputation has been built on novels concerning Roman, recent European and Scottish history. In the main, his Scottish novels highlight an uneasy relationship with the country, both socially and politically; but in *The Ragged Lion* he recreates the life of Sir Walter Scott through a rediscovered manuscript. This is the perfect vehicle for Massie's understanding and admiration of Scott. He combats Scott's public image by revealing a good and courageous man who embodies Burns' ideal.

It pleased me to throw my grounds open to the people of the neighbourhood. Nothing could have induced me to put up boards declaring them private and threatening prosecution. I saw to it only that some walks in the immediate vicinity of the house were reserved for the ladies, that they might not be alarmed by rude strangers. But for the rest, anyone who chose might wander over my land at will; I believe that was the good old way; and I often wonder how much of Burns' inspiration was due to his being able to ramble through the woods of Ballochmyle when he was but a ragged callant.

From *The Ragged Lion* Allan Massie

Massie enters Scott's conscience, revealing 'the most thoroughly Scottish of our great men' whose considerations are as much for others as for himself, whose sense of community and order drive everything he does. He is annoyed at James Hogg's lack of historical awareness and takes his publisher's and printer's debts as his own, refusing all offers of help, including a newspaper subscription to be raised in his benefit. Scott turns down honours, and is driven by a personal honesty and a belief in what is right.

A humanitarian impulse drives Massie's other works. His European novels, from *The Death of Men*, based on the murder of Aldo Moro, through *A Question of Loyalties* and *The Sins of the Father* reveal the ways in which politics can twist humanity, betray decency and use duty to deceive morality and reason. None of these issues is clear-cut. There are no extremes. Massie's strength lies in the way he puts fallible individuals in mortally difficult situations and through their foibles and misunderstandings, their loyalties to family and friends, through changing political tides and opinions, these individuals are twisted into deceit and betrayal.

On 1 July 1999 the first Scottish Parliament in almost three hundred years was convened on Edinburgh's Mound. There were fanfares and processions, sedate flag-waving crowds, speeches and recitations. But the day found its focus in an iconic moment that would forever define the day: a moment that everyone would remember.

The song is an anthem that has inspired and sustained many with a sentiment we instinctively accept as our own and know to be true.

Chris Dolan said, 'If we're looking for a national anthem, it should be *A Man's a Man*. We all know the final chorus, we all know the little bits you sing in the middle and it's got a fantastic tune. It's also got meaning, and a sentiment which nobody in their right minds could possibly disagree with.'

Commenting on when the Assembly joined in the last verse, Andrew O'Hagan: 'If I had to find one thing that made me in love with Scotland, and I'm not always in love with it, but one of the things that I'm always in love with is the tradition of idealism, of wanting things to be better, the quality of dreaming. And by singing that song at the opening of the parliament it was sending out a message: if we fail it'll be because of an insufficiency of dreaming.'

Burns bequeathed a powerful idealistic statement of how we should live our lives. It's been our first principle of social justice and it has permeated our writing since its publication. But the sentiments haven't been reflected in society. O'Hagan's right. It's time we took up the challenge, rather than have it remind us of our failure.

Is there for honest poverty
That hings his head, an' a' that?
The coward slave, we pass him by –
We dare be poor for a' that!
For a' that, an' a' that,
Our toils obscure, an' a' that
The rank is but the guinea stamp
The man's the gowd for a' that.   gold

What though on hamely fare we dine,
Wear hoddin grey, an' a' that?   coarse woollen cloth
Gie fools their silks and knaves their wine –
A man's a man for a' that.
For a' that, an' a' that,
Their tinsel show, an' a' that,
The honest man, tho' e'er sae poor,
Is king o' men for a' that.

Ye see yon birkie ca'd 'a lord',   fellow called
Wha struts, an' stares, an' a' that?
Tho' hundreds worship at his word,
He's but a cuif for a' that.   idiot
For a' that, an' a' that,
The man o' independent mind,
He looks an' laughs at a' that.

A prince can mak a belted knight,
A marquis, duke an' a' that!

But an honest man's aboon his might –
Guid faith, he maunna fa' that!   must not
For a' that, an' a' that,
Their dignities, an' a' that,
The pith o' sense and pride o' worth
Are higher rank than a' that.

Then let us pray that come it may
(As come it will for a' that)
That Sense and Worth o'er a' the earth,
Shall bear the gree an a' that.   take first place
For a' that, an a' that,
It's comin yet for a' that,
That man to man, the world o'er
Shall brithers be for a' that.
                    A Man's a Man Robert Burns

Other Worlds

I must explain that I departed this life nearly five years ago. But I did not altogether depart this world. There were those odd things still to be done which one's executors can never do properly . . . Lots of business except, of course, on Sundays and Holidays of Obligation, plenty to take an interest in for the time being.

From *The Portobello Road* Muriel Spark

Everyone is superstitious. We may be uneasy about walking under a ladder, spilling salt or putting new shoes on the table; we may live at 12a rather than 13, try not to break mirrors, walk on cracks in the pavement or stir our tea anti-clockwise.

These inexplicable little rituals are remnants of a belief system which embraces the supernatural in ways religion never would sanction. But, they're tenacious and have persisted throughout Scotland for centuries.

Many of these habits have to do with work, and the more hazardous the trade, the more likely it is the tradition will linger. In fishing communities the sight of certain people will make the crew go home. Certain animals cannot be mentioned at sea. One's wife or a minister are not welcome on board and cannot even be referred to; the boat must leave the harbour by a certain route. Yet fishing communities, especially in the north-east of Scotland, are generally devoutly religious.

Many trades had secret societies whose rites were protected. Freemasonry has expanded beyond its professional boundaries, and the coming of the tractor made the Horseman's Grip and Word redundant, but there are still initiation ceremonies for apprentices and trade secrets are guarded.

Charms were used to ward off evil and are now openly sold as jewellery, though making a profit from a charm negated its effect. Rowan trees still grow in many gardens, especially in country areas, where they were believed to keep fairies away. Horsehoes are hung outside doors for the same reason. No fairy would pass cold iron, which is still a source of locks and handles. Money given to babies bought their souls for God and silver would ensure someone with second sight could pass on their gift without interference.

Coinneach Odhar, Kenneth Mackenzie, also called the Brahan Seer, is the best known of the many Highland prophets, having apparently predicted railways, the military occupation of the Highlands, the Clearances, the Caledonian Canal and the extinction of the Earls of Seaforth. Some of his other predictions have yet to be fulfilled: 'When there shall be two churches in Ferrintosh, and a hand with two thumbs in I-Stianna, two brides at Sguideal, and a man with two navels at Dunean, soldiers will come from Tarradale on a chariot without a horse or a bridle, which will leave the Muir of Ord a wilderness.'

Second sight is associated with death. The visit of a stranger indicates the boundaries between this life and another are about to be broken. My cousins tell of a woman in black whom no one had seen before or since who turned up at my aunt's door in Oban two days before my father was killed on his way home from work in Fife. And the sight of someone near his home when he is known to be ill in bed or in hospital is said to presage his death.

While ghosts are unusual in the Highlands, Lowland Scotland abounds with haunted places. There are mounds where fairies live and the majority of what have become known as urban myths involve death or a mysterious apparition. The Loch Ness Monster is the best known of the many kelpies and water spirits which have inhabited our rivers and lochs for centuries. Adamnan tells us Columba saw the monster. Some take a human shape on land, but most make their presence known by appearing and disappearing, usually at twilight, which in Scots is called 'gloaming' and in Gaelic 'the mouth of night'.

Scottish writers, we are told, twin opposites. This unexplained phenomenon makes sense only if it's seen as a symptom, for the oppositions then become evidence rather than a consequence. Perhaps it suggests a lack of national identity, that we are both Scots and British, or it could suggest a confused identity. The aspects of national identity which serve other nations, language and traditional arts, have been undervalued and ignored here, considered unsophisticated, causing us to distort and fail to appreciate them, minimising their impact in an attempt to make them acceptable to people other than ourselves.

It could also mean that our personal identity is confused, that the oppositions are within us. Some of our greatest literature has explored the concept of identity, how it can be shaped, lost or destroyed. These explorations have brought us into contact with other worlds. Superstition is the acceptable face of a place where the real meets the unreal, where good battles with evil, where our fantasies become our fears and where we are forced to confront ourselves as we really are.

Our experience of nature and our own changing bodies tell us nothing is permanent. In the earliest, pre-literate times this idea was the basis of self-knowledge, and nature informed our early poets.

> Father, do not allow thunder and lightning.
> lest we be shattered by its fear and its fire.
>> From *Prayer from Protection*
>> *from Lightning* attrib. Columba

'If you go right back to the beginning of things,' says Kenneth White, 'you have the shaman, and he's the man who makes the connection between the small world of the social group and the large world of the universe. He's going to use all kinds of methods to transport the mind – he'll dance like a bird, he'll sing weird poems, use strange music, and so on.

'But it's a wider real world he's transporting them into; and every person in the tribe is invited to leave the social group, to go out into the wider world and then come back. But gradually the wider world becomes interpreted simply as another world, then it becomes a fantasy world; and the original journey, which was towards an expansion into the wider world, becomes a journey into a fantasy world of fiction.'

The tradition of invoking other worlds is older than literature itself, and Scotland has a rich store of folklore which relies on the idea of encountering strangers, someone from another world, or journeying into other worlds, journeys that change the people who make them, or from which they may never return:

> 'O what hills are yon, yon pleasant hills,
>   That the sun shines sweetly on?'
> 'O yon are the hills of heaven,' he said,
>   Where you will never win.'
>
> From *The Daemon Lover* (Anon.)

Ballads learned orally are still being sung and passed on today, so in that sense they are part of contemporary literature, even though they were regarded as old songs when they were first transcribed in the eighteenth century. Some go back to prehistory, while others record real events, people and places. Their influence on Scottish poetry has been absolute. Their magic is both linguistic and narrative. The precision and directness of the language is inimitable. Any words of more than three syllables are place names; and the language not only carries the tune and text, but is the basis of candour. There are no superfluous diversions. The stories proceed directly to their point and the narrative climax is soon reached.

Emily Lyle cites a number of examples of prehistoric ballads which involve the real meeting the unreal, battles between good and evil or change and transformation. The earliest reference to a real character is Thomas of Erceldoune, known as Thomas the Rhymer, who lived in the Borders in the thirteenth century. True Thomas was tempted away from the real world by the enchantingly beautiful Queen of the Faeries and lived with her in her underground realm for seven years.

> True Thomas lay on Huntlie Bank
> A ferlie he spied wi' his ee   marvel
> And there he saw a lady bright,
> Come riding down by the Eildon Tree.

> 'Harp and carp, Thomas,' she said,
> 'Harp and carp along wi' me,   play harp and sing
> And if ye dare to kiss my lips
> Sure of your bodie I will be.'
>
> From *Thomas the Rhymer* (Anon.)

Thomas mistakes the Queen of Elfland for the Queen of Heaven and though warned of the consequences, nevertheless cannot prevent himself from kissing her, which may suggest warnings of another sort, for Biblical connections are never far away.

The supernatural world and the consequences of Hell are constant ballad features. If the narrator fails to tell us directly, murdered bodies return from the dead to reveal treachery, lovers who were separated by circumstances, personal whim or cruel parents are reunited in death and guilt forces the wicked to call for their victims' forgiveness, usually from the grave. Forgiveness is rarely offered, far less granted and relief comes only when life is ended. In *The Great Silkie of Sule Skerray*, a woman is impregnated by a night visitor – 'I am a man upon the land/And I am a silkie on the sea' – who will return to take his son. The ballad is the basis of an Eric Linklater story:

He was not only naked, but obviously robust, brown-hued, and extremely hairy. He sat on the very edge of the rock, dangling his legs over the sea, and down his spine ran a ridge of hair like the dark stripe on a donkey's back, and on his shoulder-blades grew patches of hair like the wings of a bird.

Unable in her disappointment to be sensible and leave at once, she lingered for a moment and saw to her relief that he was not quite naked. He wore trousers of a dark brown colour, very low at the waist, but sufficient to cover his haunches. Even so, even with that protection for her modesty, she could not stay and read biology in his company.

From *Sealskin Trousers* Eric Linklater

In *Night Visiting Songs* consequences generally follow actions, though many are simple celebrations – 'But I will climb wi' the greatest pleasure/ Noo that I've laid wi' my ain true love' – just as ballads with a riddle at their heart are in the main successfully answered by young girls foolish enough to promise themselves to an older man, often the Devil in disguise, who challenges them to explain a series of conundrums. He's a familiar figure in Scottish folklore; and the sense of what is real and what is unreal, the practical and the fantastic, runs through the whole of Scottish literature and is one of its abiding themes. The real subject of the ballad is life itself and at the heart of many songs is an individual warning. Ballads, in the main, were the work of folk whose experience was bound by parish borders. Danger lay 'faur, faur ower yon high, high hill'. So the warnings were meant to be heeded.

Fantasy writing can be a form of escapism, a warning or a harbinger of doom, revealing what will happen if we don't do what we're told. But, at its best, fantasy can also expose the world we inhabit, maybe even the place we inhabit too.

Journeys to the other world were a dangerous business and the knowledge found there was supposed to be a closely guarded secret. Robert Kirk was the Presbyterian minister of Aberfoyle. He supervised the production of a Gaelic Bible in London and translated the metrical psalms into Gaelic. Kirk alleged he was taken to fairyland and shown the fairies' secrets, but he broke trust with the other world by publishing *The Secret Commonwealth of Elves, Fauns and Fairies* in 1691. Its inhabitants were so angry they stole him away. He was never seen again but his soul is reputedly imprisoned beneath the roots of a pine tree, which tops Doune Hill in the Trossachs.

The Siths, or Fairies . . . are said to be of a middle nature betwixt man and angel, as were demons thought to be of old, of intelligent studious spirits, and light changeable bodies (like those called astral), somewhat of the nature of a condensed cloud, and best seen in twilight. These bodies be so pliable through the subtlety of the spirits that agitate them, that they can make them appear and disappear at pleasure.

From *The Secret Commonwealth of Elves,*
Fauns and Fairies Robert Kirk

This was a time when Presbyterian extremists were committed to the eradication of witchcraft. There are few examples of men being burned as sorcerers; but because of The Fall and the Devil's known liking for women, it was assumed they would be more susceptible to his charms and advances. In 1597 King James VI had written *Daemonologie*, a treatise in the form of a dialogue, detailing a variety of fears, mostly concerning female sexuality.

The fearefull aboundinge at this time in this countrie, of these detestable slaves of the Devill, the Witches or enchanters, hath moved me (beloved reader) to dispatch in post, this following treatise of mine, not in any way (as I protest) to serve for a shew of my learning and ingine, but onely (mooved of conscience) to preasse thereby, so farre as I can, to resolve the doubting harts of many; both that such assaultes of Sathan are most certainly practized, and that the instrumentes thereof, merits most severely to be punished: against the damnable opinions of two principally in our age, whereof the one called SCOT an Englishman, is not ashamed in publike print to deny, that ther can be such a

thing as Witchcraft: and so mainteines the old error of the
Sadducees, in denying of spirits.

From Daemonologie James VI

And twenty years later George Sinclair, Glasgow University's
Professor of Experimental Philosophy, published *Satan's Invisible
World Discovered*, revealing instances of supernatural events and
apparitions, including evidence from witchcraft trials.

The best known was when Sir George Maxwell of Pollok met the
Devil and his Hags. Annabil Stewart testified that 'in Harvest last,
the Devil in the shape of a black man had come to her Mothers
house, and requited the Deponent to give herself up to him',
promising 'anything that was good'. The girl got a new coat and a
new name; the Devil called her Annippy, having nipped her arm,
which was sore for half an hour. Annabil got off, but her mother
was burned on her daughter's testimony. It would take a whole
summer's day, she said, to relate the many meetings that took
place between her mother and the Devil.

The last Scottish trial and execution for witchcraft took place in
Dornoch in 1722, fourteen years before laws governing witchcraft
were repealed and almost fifty years before James Hogg was born.
Hogg was the first Scottish writer to put the fantastic at the centre
of his vision, and though it wasn't critically recognised for over a
hundred years, his novel *The Private Memoirs and Confessions of a
Justified Sinner* is now seen as one of the great masterpieces of
Scottish writing. It is also, I believe, a masterpiece of world
literature.

Hogg was born at Ettrickhall farmhouse near Selkirk in 1770,
down the glen from Walter Scott in Abbotsford. His mother,
Margaret Laidlaw, his uncle and elder brother contributed to
Scott's *The Minstrelsy of the Scottish Borders* and Hogg maintained
his mother's ballads, songs and stories 'formed the groundwork of
my intellectual being'.

Hogg was seven when he began work as a shepherd. He later
described a time when he went barefoot and wore a ragged coat,

living in a roughly built bothy, not much more than a hole in the ground. He had to stoop to enter and couldn't stand inside. With no bed except for the rushes, he shared this hut with cattle and sheep.

In a memoir, he records the events that made him a writer. It all started in 1797, the year after Burns died. Hogg was twenty-seven years old.

One day during that summer a half daft man, named John Scott, came to me on the hill, and to amuse me repeated Tam O'Shanter. I was delighted! I was far more than delighted – I was ravished! I cannot describe my feelings, but, in short, before Jock Scott left me, I could recite the poem from beginning to end, and it has been my favourite poem ever since. He told me it was made by one Robert Burns, the sweetest poet that ever was born; but that he was now dead, and his place would never be supplied. He told me all about him, how he was born on the 25th of January, bred a ploughman, how many beautiful songs and poems he com- posed, and that he had died last harvest, on the 21st of August.

From *Memorials of James Hogg the Ettrick Shepherd* James Hogg

Tam O'Shanter is our best-known piece of supernatural writing; and while we may find it over-familiar, there is no doubting its impact on Hogg. Burns wrote the poem in December 1790, in a single sitting at Ellisland. It was first published in the *Edinburgh Herald* in March the following year and was included in the second Edinburgh edition of Burns poems published from Allan Ramsay's former bookshop in the High Street in 1793 by the notoriously stingy William Creech. Four years later it had entered the oral tradition.

It was a turning point for Hogg. He decided to become a writer, even though he described himself as illiterate. He had wee bits of schooling, something like six months in all, where he was intro-duced to the Bible, the Metrical Psalms of David, the Proverbs of Solomon and the Shorter Catechism. When he was six his father went bankrupt and James was put out to service with a succession of masters. By the time he became a shepherd what little he'd learned had gone.

Hogg's biographer Karl Miller describes the term illiterate as then meaning untutored or uncultivated. 'Hogg learned to read and write in his teens,' he says in *Electric Shepherd*, 'and caught up fairly soon. In time, he was climbing the hill with slates on which to compose, and with an ink bottle for good measure, stuck in a hole in his waistcoat, together with a cork, a piece of string, the stump of a pen, or a sheet or two of paper folded and stitched. He went on composing in this way, and would later claim to be nothing without the slate.'

He started to write around 1793: 'I about this time began to read with considerable attention; – and no sooner did I begin to read so as to understand, than, rather prematurely, I began to write,'

Hogg spent his life believing he shared a birthday with Burns and only learned this wasn't the case two years before his death. He also came to admire Burns' widow, and from his hole on the hill saw himself as Burns' successor: 'I too was born on the 25th of January, and I have more time to read and compose than any ploughman could have, and can sing more old songs than ever a ploughman could in the world. But then I wept again because I could not write.'

Though his verse exploits Borders folklore and tradition, it took Hogg a while to find his feet as a poet. He sent ballads he'd collected to Scott, moved to Edinburgh, launched a collection of songs and started a magazine, which lasted a year. Disappointed by his failure to imitate Burns' success, in the last issue he published a *Memoir of the Author's Life*, where he paraded himself as The Ettrick Shepherd, an illiterate genius seeking his fortune in the arts. This was a role he lived to regret.

In 1807, he published a collection of his own ballads, and, with

Scott's narrative verse at the height of its popularity, wrote *The Queen's Wake*, which purported to be a series of poems recited by different bards in competition before Mary, Queen of Scots. *Kilmeny* was among the most popular items.

Hogg said the poem came to him in a dream. It describes how a pure-hearted maiden is spirited to the realm of the fairies where she is shown the future of Scotland. Years later, magically unchanged, she returns.

Late, late in the gloamin when all was still,
When the fringe was red on the westlin hill,
The wood was sere, the moon i' the wane,
The reek o' the cot hung over the plain,
Like a little wee cloud in the world its lane,
When the ingle lowed with an eiry leme,   eerie gleam
Late, late in the gloaming Kimeny came hame!

From *Kilmeny* James Hogg

The Queen's Wake was published in 1813 and not only made Hogg's name, but led Blackwood's to take him onto their list. This was where he met his friends, Professor John Wilson, the pseudonymous Christopher North, and Scott's son-in-law John Gibson Lockhart. Wilson's influence on Scottish literature was pretty dismal, other than establishing and fertilising a garden where kale could grow. He was mainly responsible, though Lockhart helped out, for mimicking Hogg in the *Noctes Ambrosianae*, a series of essays and supposedly overheard conversations where Hogg is portrayed as an ignorant simpleton given to meaningless discourse, tackling subjects far above his intellectual level and making a fool of himself in the process.

No matter how easily Hogg accepted the role, the fact that he did so says more about him than it does about the perpetrators. The men were divided by social difference, so perhaps he had little alternative, especially since Blackwood himself seems to have joined in the sport. Hogg was still living on the hill in his thirties.

How could such distinguished intellects have anything in common with a man who had lived in a hole in the ground and wrote a *Shepherd's Guide*, describing the best way to geld sheep by biting their balls.

The continual travesty angered Hogg's wife as well as many of his friends and though he complained about his views being misrepresented, he accepted it was part of an elaborate game. And there does appear to be a personal friendship and collaboration between the three; given the length of their acquaintance and the closeness of their working relationship, how could it be otherwise?

Perhaps the best indication comes from an outside observer. In Sir William Allan's painting, *The Celebration of the Birthday of James Hogg*, a fair-haired, rosy-cheeked Wilson is at the centre of the picture, in white shirt and trousers, raising a quaich in Hogg's direction. He is surrounded by the great and the good, by Scott and his publisher James Ballantyne, the painters Alexander Nasmyth and William Nicholson. Allan himself is there. Lockhart stands above the group, smoking a churchwarden pipe. Hogg is at the edge of the table, slightly apart from the others, dressed in black, face flushed, hand at his head, in antic pose.

The Blackwoods circle helped to stereotype Hogg as the Ettrick Shepherd, which ensured he was seen as a curious eccentric, the writer of occasional verse and country stories. Hogg's poems can be very energetic, as well as experimental, and use a wide range of voices, while his stories give the feeling of being narrated rather than written. Events occur naturally with little preamble or artifice, details of character and background are given as they occur or appear relevant, and incidents are rarely signalled. Hogg takes the position of a disingenuous narrator, who is as amazed by the events as his reader, especially where a supernatural element is involved. He often gives a personal assurance that the narrative is true, that he can offer personal testimony to certain aspects and he often halts the narrative in a perfectly natural way to explain events or detail their relevance.

'For him, the folktale world and the world of the supernatural has a truth to it that is very reliable,' says novelist Margaret Elphinstone, 'and he stays in that broader world of folktale all his life. He always had it accessible and it shows in his poetry and fiction.'

At the heart of Hogg's writing is a quest for identity, the idea that nothing is fixed, that we can inhabit contradictions and, terrifyingly, that they can inhabit us. He teaches us that one thing or person can be two and two can be one. This shifting duality not only gives us an immediate access to and understanding of Hogg's condition in Edinburgh, which allowed him to be accepted as a writer and simultaneously considered a fool, but it allows us to enter his work linguistically and socially.

Arthur's Seat towers above Edinburgh with an ancient and primordial inscrutability, suggesting something dark and untamed at the heart of the capital. And to follow the sinuous path along Salisbury Crags is to trace Hogg's own footsteps; it was a walk he often took. This is where one of the most memorable passages in *The Memoirs and Confessions of a Justified Sinner* takes place. The novel's main character is split, and on Salisbury Crags meets his diabolical second self:

He saw delineated in the cloud, the shoulders, arms and features of a human being of the most dreadful aspect . . . Its eyes gleamed on him through the mist, while every furrow of its hideous brow frowned deep as the ravines on the brow of the hill. George started, and his hair stood up in bristles as he gazed on his horrible monster. He saw every feature and every line of the face distinctly as it gazed on him with an intensity that was hardly brookable. Its eyes were fixed on him, in the same manner as those of some carnivorous animal fixed on its prey; and yet there was fear and trembling in these unearthly features, as plainly depicted as murderous malice. The giant apparition seemed sometimes to be cowering down as in terror, so that nothing but its brow and eyes were seen; still these never turned one moment from their object – again it rose imperceptibly up, and began to approach with great caution; and, as it neared, the dimensions of its form lessened, still continuing, however, far above the natural size.

From *The Private Memoirs and Confessions of a Justified Sinner* James Hogg

The sinner of *The Memoirs and Confessions of a Justified Sinner* is convinced he's one of God's chosen and therefore beyond blame, an arrogant delusion that leads to murder and insanity. Other writers, notably Burns, lampooned this holy hypocrisy, but Hogg had a much deeper insight, turning it into something far more fearful.

Hogg took the heart of Burns' satire and carried Holy Willie's thinking to its logical conclusion, showing us what Willie was like with the satire removed. But whatever he may be on the outside, Robert Wringhim is no hypocrite. He believes he is right, that God tells him so and, in effect, he has God in his pocket. His story is consequently psychologically precise. It is an accurate and detailed case history of a kind of madness, of a moral destruction.

Ian Rankin points to the novel's contemporary relevance: 'The terrific ambiguity at the heart of the *Confessions* is this idea that you're never sure if the devil is really a devil or part of the hero's subconscious,' he says. 'Is it a physical person? Is evil physical and out there or is the potential for evil within us? And that's an ongoing debate. Every age has its own manifestation of this question: what makes us do good things and what makes us do bad things? We have the capability to be good living individuals, but we have the capability equally to do harm and it's a war within us about doing right or wrong.'

'It's a terrifying story about a serial killer,' says novelist Alan Bissett. 'It takes huge risks with narrative structure, with register, with voice, and it really sets the template for all these novels that came after it.'

Dostoevsky came after it, Stevenson too, but it's impossible to say if they were aware of Hogg's *Sinner*. And even though it's now considered to be the most significant Scottish novel of the nineteenth century, it was published anonymously and attracted little attention at the time. The book's rehabilitation began in 1947, when André Gide called it 'an extraordinary achievement'. It had been reprinted once in the previous century. But Hogg provided the impetus for Scottish fiction's next major development. His ideas would be famously explored a generation later by Robert Louis Stevenson.

Tam O'Shanter is the best known piece of Scottish supernatural writing, so familiar now that its subtleties and initial message have been obliterated. And the same is true of *The Strange Case of Dr Jekyll and Mr Hyde*. Because of their familiarity, it's easy to overlook the fact that both pieces reveal a world which runs parallel to our own, that there are points where the two worlds mingle and that one can spill into the other. As a means of social control, this idea is very powerful and clearly goes a long way to explaining the power of the Kirk, but it is also an imaginative springboard whose reverberations are still being felt today.

As a young man, Stevenson enjoyed something of a double life. By day he was the dutiful son of a middle-class family living in Edinburgh's New Town. By night he would roam the Old Town streets in search of alternative entertainment. In this other world, buoyed up with drink, he enjoyed the excitement of a middle-class boy who mixes with petty thieves, drunks and prostitutes, the kind of social elements Victorian society feared, tried to save or strove to keep in check. The struggle between good and evil is one of Stevenson's continuing preoccupations.

The novelist, Donna Tartt, sees Jekyll and Hyde as prophetic: 'The nature of the urban life is secrecy. It's very easy in the twentieth century to have a double life. He was really anticipating all sorts of things, including the hideous world of the serial killer.'

The Strange Case of Dr Jekyll and Mr Hyde was supposedly influenced by the real life story of Deacon William Brodie. A respectable cabinetmaker and town official by day, by night he terrorised the town with a series of burglaries. Caught for a heist on the Excise Office, where the total haul was £16/0/0, Brodie tried to explain the evil side of his divided self by saying his 'maniac brother had slipped his chain'. Condemned to death he tried to cheat the noose by wearing a metal collar and bribing the hangman. The plan failed.

Stevenson had written a play about Deacon Brodie, but he dreamed the Jekyll story. It was, he said 'conceived, written, rewritten, rewritten and printed' in ten weeks during the autumn of 1885. Stevenson's health was poor and he had perpetual money worries. His friend, the electrical engineer Henry Fleeming Jenkin, the subject of Stevenson's only biography, had recently died and he was anxious to find something that would both free him from the demands of the Jenkin biography and restore the critical success of *Treasure Island*, published two years earlier. The dream came after he had spent two days looking for a plot of any sort.

'I had long been trying to write a story on this subject,' he recalled in *A Chapter on Dreams*, 'to find a body, a vehicle for that strong sense of man's double being which must at times come in upon and overwhelm the mind of every thinking creature . . . on the second night I dreamed the scene at the window, and a scene afterwards split in two, in which Hyde, pursued for some crime, took the powder and underwent the change in the presence of his pursuers. All the rest was made awake and consciously.'

'Dr Jekyll and Mr Hyde is a nightmare from which he awoke screaming,' says Donna Tartt. 'In a way he was dreaming the twentieth century, the duality of man, the urban nature of the divided self.'

The novel tells of how the respectable Dr Jekyll believed personal identity could be divided. Jekyll mirrors the Justified Sinner insofar as his education and position give him a superior social standing. In other words, he can be seen as a member of society's elect. Stevenson rooted the story in a reality which adds a shocking and original dimension. Jekyll recognises his own duality and his experiments were meant to remove rather than to release his other self. Personality, he thought, could be divided many times.

When he finds pleasure in slipping the bands of respectability, and believes he has found the cure which will make him complete, which will offer release from himself rather than deepen his entrapment, his experience mirrors precisely that of many alcoholics and drug addicts. Obsessives everywhere will respond to Dr Jekyll's thinking: having tried what the individual sees as every possible personal solution, from control to abstinence, the fear that the demon will return and take control is never far away.

> With every day . . . I drew steadily nearer the truth: that man is not truly one, but truly two . . . I had learned to dwell with pleasure . . . on the thought of the separation of these elements. If each, I told myself, could but be housed in separate identities, life would be relieved of all that was unbearable; the unjust might go his way, delivered from the aspirations and remorse of his more upright twin; and the just could walk steadfastly and securely on his upward path, doing the good things in which he found his pleasure, and no longer exposed to disgrace and penitence by the hands of this extraneous evil. It was the curse of mankind that these incongruous faggots were thus bound together – that in the agonised womb of consciousness these polar twins should be continuously struggling.
>
> From *The Strange Case of Dr Jekyll and
> Mr Hyde* Robert Louis Stevenson

Ian Rankin sees in Jekyll and Hyde the nature of humanity: 'The fact that we're only one step away from the cave, that all those primordial urges are still there within us. We've got anger, we've got jealousy, we've got all the rage you'll ever need bottled up within us to make us social human beings. But it doesn't take much for it to go.'

He put the glass to his lips and drank at one gulp. A cry followed; he reeled, staggered, clutched at the table and held on, staring with injected eyes, gasping with open mouth; and as I looked there came, I thought a change – he seemed to swell – his face became suddenly black, and his features seemed to melt and alter – and the next moment I had sprung to my feet and leaped back against the wall, my arm raised to shield me from that prodigy, my mind submerged in terror.

From The Strange Case of Dr Jekyll and
Mr Hyde Robert Louis Stevenson

When a character transforms from one world to another, or from one state to another, he strangely and brilliantly remains the same. What lies below the surface is exposed; and if he is without redeeming features, and cannot maintain qualities such as love, inspiration, beauty, joy and truth, the things that make us human, then his position is truly hopeless. With nothing to combat evil, malevolence will triumph; 'which is why Hyde is probably the most despicable character who ever appeared in fiction,' says Margaret Elphinstone.

The Strange Case of Dr Jekyll and Mr Hyde has achieved mythological status. It has been filmed many times and other novelists have taken up its theme. People who have never read the book know the story. Stevenson's stories, even his adventure stories, present startling oppositions – Jim Hawkins and Long John Silver, David Balfour and Alan Breck Stewart – but here the opposition is within oneself; and the similarities with Hogg's *Confessions* are striking. Neither book offers a fixed definition of truth, nor a moral conclusion.

The only active ingredient of Dr Jekyll's potion mentioned is the drug alcohol, the traditional method Scots have used to explore the boundaries between fantasy and reality. Stevenson would often leave meetings by saying that he was 'off to buy pencils'. In his autobiography, the Court of Session judge, Lord Guthrie, recalls,

'When I joined the Speculative Society the practice was to adjourn between the essay and the debate "to buy pencils" which novices were amazed to find meant beer at Rutherford's public house.' His lordship recalls they sold coffee, which had been made in a kettle 'according to the recipe in the Cape Wars early last century – vile stuff'.

Rutherford's is a Drummond Street pub, a stone's throw from Edinburgh University's Old College. Writing to his friend and executor Charles Baxter from the 'Yacht Casco, at sea, near the Paumotus 7 a.m., September 6, 1888, with a dreadful pen', Stevenson recalled that the previous night 'was as warm as milk, and all of a sudden I had a flash of – Drummond Street. It came to me like a flash of lightning: I simply returned thither, and into the past. And when I remembered all I hoped and feared as I pickled about Rutherford's in the rain and the east wind; how I feared I should make a mere shipwreck, and yet timidly hoped not; how I feared I should never have a friend, far less a wife, and yet passionately hoped I might; how I hoped (if I did not take to drink) I should possibly write one little book, etc. etc. And then now – what a change! I feel somehow as if I should like the incident set upon a brass plate at the corner of that dreary thoroughfare for all students to read, poor devils, when their hearts are down.'

Conan Doyle knew the pub and mentions it in a story, *The First Operation*. Barrie may well have known it too, but his account of meeting Stevenson is fiction. He recalled a chance encounter in Princes Street and how Stevenson took him by the arm 'away from the Humanities class at the University to something he assured me was more humane – a howff called Rutherford's'.

Barrie had been asked to contribute to a book, *I Can Remember Robert Louis Stevenson*. His contribution began, 'As I never saw Stevenson face to face, I have no right to be in this volume.' He ends with the observation that had Stevenson lived another year, they would have met. Barrie was planning to visit Stevenson in Samoa when he got news of his death.

In a letter to the editor, he composed the fictitious meeting, ending with Stevenson selling his velvet jacket for more bottles of Chambertin and one or the other singing. He left Rutherford's in the blinding snow, pursued by Stevenson to his lodgings in Frederick Street. Years later, he saw a newspaper portrait and recognised his friend of the night. 'Alas. Heigho,' he ends. 'It might have been.'

We don't know what lesson Barrie would have taken from Stevenson, but he was clearly attracted to the supernatural. And though his books and plays are often light in touch, there is a darker side to Barrie, which rarely appears in his prose and is often masked by a sentimental interpretation of his work.

Barrie began by recreating the stories his mother told him. With Ian Maclaren (pseudonym of the Rev. John Watson) and S.R. Crockett, Barrie was part of the Kailyard school, a commercially successful movement which exploited all that was mawkishly sentimental and escapist in Scottish writing. Their stories present a version of country life that city folk can enjoy. Aimed at our moral and sentimental sympathies, they show a rural idyll which was familiar enough to be funny and innocent enough to be patronised.

James Matthew Barrie was born in Kirriemuir in 1864 into a close knit and loving family. He was one of five daughters and three sons born to a linen weaver who worked from home. All the children were brought up in the Free Kirk, though their mother, Margaret Ogilvy, came from a more puritanical set, the Auld Lichts.

Mrs Barrie's favourite son, David, who was destined for the ministry, was killed in a skating accident at thirteen. She fell into an obsessive grief, which excluded her youngest son, James, who tried to replace David in his mother's affections. Margaret Ogilvy's only comfort was that in death, David would remain a boy forever. The accident and the mother's grief tore the family apart and Barrie's life was changed forever.

Like Dr Jekyll, Barrie underwent a transformation, becoming

for his mother the son that she had lost. For the rest of his life, he seems to have been obsessed with childhood and the imaginative world of prepubescent boys, and it's for his depiction of childhood that Barrie remains famous. Every year, parents take their children to see a play which has been packing theatres for a hundred years. On one level, it's a wonderful fantasy adventure; on another it's a brilliant dramatisation of our darkest fears.

Peter Pan is the story of a strange, dysfunctional boy who refuses to grow up, a boy who lures children to a place where they battle with murderous pirates and meet a morally suspect fairy. Peter first appeared in a story in *The Little White Bird*, published in 1902. The play *Peter Pan*, or *The Boy Who Wouldn't Grow Up*, was first performed at the Duke of York's Theatre, London, in 1904. Barrie's script was originally rejected because it was so elaborate. In 1904, plays generally did not involve flying and frequent and major scene changes. In 1906, the section of *The Little White Bird* that originated *Peter Pan* was published separately as a book called *Peter Pan in Kensington Gardens*. Finally, Barrie turned the play into a novel called *Peter and Wendy*, published in 1911.

The name Wendy didn't exist till Barrie created it from his own nickname. Stevenson's friend and collaborator W.E. Henley, whose physical incapacity made him the model for Long John Silver, had a daughter Margaret who called Barrie Friendy-Wendy. And the portrait of Wendy is said to owe much to Barrie's mother, who raised her younger brother.

Peter Pan evolved from stories Barrie told Sylvia Llewellyn Davies's five young sons. She was the daughter of the novelist George du Maurier, and a motherly figure, with whom Barrie had a long friendship. Barrie's wife Mary began an affair with the writer Gilbert Cannan in 1909 and their marriage ended in divorce, amid doubts as to whether it had been consummated.

When Sylvia Llewellyn Davies and her husband died, Barrie became their sons' guardian. George, one of the sons, died in the

First World War and Michael was drowned with a friend in Oxford. Michael's death was a deep blow to Barrie. Peter, who became a publisher, committed suicide in 1960.

'All children, except one, grow up. They soon know that they will grow up,' is how the story begins in the Darlings' Bloomsbury flat, which is visited by Peter Pan. He has run away from home to avoid growing up. Like his attendant fairy Tinker Bell, he can fly and teaches the skill to the three Darling children.

Donna Tartt sees the play as being centred on changelessness: 'It's a book about death, mortality and time. But it's also a book about incorruptibility, about a sort of brightness that really verges on divinity.'

Peter Pan lures children from the safety of their beds to the moral chaos of Never Land, a magical place beyond the stars where Peter lives with the Lost Boys, protected by a tribe of Red Indians. Wendy becomes mother to the boys. When Peter is away, the pirate Captain Hook captures her and her 'family'. They are saved from having to walk the plank by Peter's bravery. Hook is eaten by his nemesis, a crocodile that has swallowed a ticking clock. Peter takes Wendy and her brothers home to Bloomsbury, but declines an offer of adoption from Mrs Darling. Having tried to bar Wendy from going into the house, he comes to the window to say goodbye. Mrs Darling stretches her arms to him.

'Keep back, lady,' he says, 'No one is going to catch me and make me a man.'

Wendy promises to visit him each year to do the spring-cleaning.

'In an obvious way,' says Margaret Elphinstone, 'the story of Peter takes us back to the tradition of fantastic journeys. Never Land is a quite explicit faerie kingdom. But there is a profound difference. Travellers don't go there to be changed. Like Kilmeny, they remain as they are, forever.'

Playwright Stuart Paterson, who recently adapted the play, thinks *Peter Pan* is 'the greatest piece of Scottish art there is, and certainly by a long, long way our greatest play.

'Peter Pan is happy when he's terrifying other people or when he's thrilling other people or when he's escaping into thrill and adventure. If he stays still for a second, he's utterly miserable. That's the hell he's in; and that's why it's a really scary play to stage and to do. You need an actor playing Peter Pan who understands there's something almost mischievous and terrifying about this character; and if you miss that you miss Barrie's point, and you miss the incredible power of his play.'

'Who is Captain Hook?' he asked with interest when she spoke of the arch enemy.

'Don't you remember,' she asked, amazed, 'how you killed him and saved all our lives?'

'I forget them after I kill them,' he replied carelessly.

When she expressed a doubtful hope that Tinker Bell would be glad to see her he said, 'Who is Tinker Bell?'

'O Peter,' she said, shocked; but even when she explained he could not remember.

'There are such a lot of them,' he said. 'I expect she is no more.'

I expect he was right, for fairies don't live long, but they are so little that a short time seems a good while to them.

Wendy was pained too to find that the past year was but as yesterday to Peter; it had seemed such a long year of waiting to her. But he was exactly as fascinating as ever, and they had a lovely spring cleaning in the little house on the tree tops.

Next year he did not come for her. She waited in a new frock because the old one simply would not meet; but he never came.

From *Peter and Wendy* J.M. Barrie

The play was a huge success and has been adapted for various media many times, most familiarly in the Disney versions. But ten years after it was premiered, the generation who grew up with Peter's cheery notion that 'death is an awfully big adventure' found themselves marching to the battlefields of the First World War. Off-duty soldiers drew comfort from Never Land, a place of eternal childhood. The adventure of death – the greatest adventure of all – would guarantee eternal youth, a consolation many soldiers must have carried with them when they faced the guns.

The line was removed after the war.

Other Barrie plays such as *Dear Brutus*, produced in 1917 and *Mary Rose*, produced in 1920, can be seen as much more powerful fantasies which helped people to cope with the aftermath of war. There's a similar sense of people vanishing, or disappearing somewhere, going off while life continues. There are hints of death and eternal childhood, and poignant divisions between age and youth are openly and innocently exposed.

'We're all afraid of death,' says Stuart Paterson, 'we're all afraid of growing up, and if you don't have a religious faith, which I'm sure Barrie didn't have, we come up with all sorts of other things to take its place. Sitting in the theatre in the dark, and contemplating your own life through a brilliant piece of art is as powerful as going to church if you're a non-believer.'

'This going off to the other place, the place of faerie or imagination, that owes something to the ballad tradition, to folk tradition where this keeps happening,' says Margaret Elphinstone. 'There are two worlds and certain people move between the two, rhymers or children, there are certain privileged people who can go back and forth.'

Even in the magical world of Never Land, Barrie's adult fears are painfully expressed. To my mind, one of the most tragic lines of any play is when Peter says, 'No one must ever touch me.'

Seventy years later, fear of human contact would become a central theme for another Scottish writer. Alasdair Gray introduces a fantastical version of this condition in his novel *Lanark*. Deprived of love and sunlight, the citizens of Unthank develop a hideous skin condition called Dragonhide. Those afflicted can't be touched even if they want to be. Only love can heal them.

He began to say he was not interested in her disease but she pulled off her fur gauntlet. Surprise gagged him. He had expected dragon claws like his own, but all he could see was a perfectly shaped white little hand, the fingers tightly clenched, until she unclenched them to show the palm. He took a moment to recognise what lay on it. A mouth lay on it, grinning sarcastically. It opened and said in a tiny voice, 'You're trying to understand things, and that interests me.'

It was Sludden's voice. Lanark whispered, 'Oh, this is hell!'

Gay's hand sank to her side. He saw that the soles of her feet were an inch above the pavement. Her body dangled before him as if from a hook in her brain, her smile was vacant and silly, her jaw fell and the voice which came from the mouth was not formed by movement of tongue or lip.

From *Lanark* Alasdair Gray

'In this hell, I imagined human beings gradually turning into monsters, or devils if you like,' says Alasdair Gray, 'the transformation being slightly based upon how they were in life. There was the notion that those who'd been rather cold and stand-offish and afraid to show their feelings developed a kind of skin or carapace which makes them very spiky and dragonish. They get hot inside because they're not sharing their warmth with people outside. And eventually they explode.'

Alasdair Gray has created a book which encapsulates the entire tradition of fantasy, otherworldliness, and duality that permeates Scottish literature. *Lanark* is a wonderfully inventive and exuberant work, darkly comic and surreal. It is divided into four books, opens with an Epilogue on Book Three, contains an Index of Plagiarisms, plays with typefaces and layout, and the title pages and cover were drawn by the author, who makes an appearance in the text when he meets and converses with Lanark.

Lanark has no memory. He is displaced and impoverished when we meet him and a group of intellectuals in an art cinema café. The city he inhabits is a place where inhabitants disappear at night, where the inner city is becoming depopulated and remnants of industry rot by the river. The connection between Unthank and the reality of Glasgow lifts the book into the world of social satire and political comment. Real social problems are highlighted awhile, then disappear, emerge every now and then, but gradually fade from view.

The novel reflects the city Gray remembers in the 1940s and 1950s when the story is set. Lanark is trying to discover where he is and gradually pieces his life together. It's a journey where he encounters bureaucratic social workers and corrupt politicians, has an unhappy affair and gradually discovers, or is led to discover, the power of the Institute, an amalgam of all forms of institution, from prison to hospital, university to office.

Most senses abandoned him now. Thought and memory, stench, heat and direction dissolved and he knew nothing but pressure and duration . . . And then he felt like an infinite worm in infinite darkness, straining and straining and failing to disgorge a lump which was choking him to death.

From *Lanark* Alasdair Gray

Lanark is haunted by a vision of sunlight. At the end of the first part, Book Three, Lanark finds he's had a previous existence as Duncan Thaw, whose life is described in the middle section, Books One and Two, before we return to Unthank and the Institute in Book Four. Duncan also has a skin complaint, which makes him shy, and this affects his relationships with other people, which, in turn, makes him painfully lonely, despite a wide circle of friends. Everything in Duncan's life is pointless. He is an asthmatic mural artist, painting on walls which will be demolished.

'To me, the man's just struggling for love,' says Gray, 'to be loved by a woman, to be loved by his family. He doesn't manage to keep either, but he later discovers that he's not been unloved. He wants to be part of a healthy, sunlit city, and the book ends with the sun beginning to dawn over Unthank, even though he's about to die; so I don't see the book with a totally miserable ending.'

Lanark has had an unmitigated influence on the succeeding generation of writers. Iain Banks not only admires everything Gray has written, but thinks he is, arguably, the best Scottish writer of the twentieth century. 'Lanark absolutely stunned me,' he says. 'I read Lanark and I just thought, Wow! This is what you can do. It really opened my eyes as to what was possible in fiction. I was just amazed by it. My own novel, The Bridge, I don't think would have been anything like it turned out if it hadn't been for Lanark.'

Banks' book is not derivative of Gray. His imaginative credentials were already well established, as author of The Wasp Factory and Walk on Glass, as well as a variety of science fiction novels as Iain M. Banks. His character lives in a nightmarish world and is caught in a system of institutionalised class and economic structures, which matches Banks' political views with Gray. Banks refused to attend a party for Young British Novelists because it was hosted by Saatchi & Saatchi, whose close connections to the Conservatives were well known; he later tore up his passport in protest against the war in Iraq.

The Bridge reverses the fantasy tradition by journeying from dream to reality. The book's hero lies in a coma, his character fragmented into multiple personalities following a car crash on the Forth Road Bridge.

'It offered a wonderful structure,' says Banks. 'There are three main bits to the book and there's three main bits to the bridge. There's viaducts at either end, there's little linking bridges in between, which gave me a structure to hang the whole story, or group of stories, onto. It's a fantastic bridge he's on because he's in a coma; and, in a sense, he's constructed his own bridge. He's allowed to think; maybe it's a bridge that goes on forever. Maybe it girdles the world. So you start from one end and, eventually, you come round to the same place. All these things are symbolic of where his head is at, as he gradually works through his life and memories and tries to establish what might happen in the future, and decide whether he actually wants to come back or not.'

The road ahead cleared the cutting through the hills . . . the old rail bridge's hollow bones looked the colour of dried blood. . . . then he was aware of the truck pulling out suddenly. He sucked his breath in, stamped on the brakes, tried to swerve, but it was too late.

From *The Bridge* Iain Banks

'It's important for the protagonist to get across,' says Banks, 'because that's connecting with reality. The land on either side represents his real life, what's actually happened, though it's his choice. He might choose not to and this is part of the dynamic of the book. You're aware that he knows. He actually says, This is a dream.'

In his coma state, Banks' hero lives on a vast, seemingly endless dream version of the Forth Rail Bridge, a city of multiple levels suspended a thousand feet above the sea.

Crossing the bridge from unconsciousness, Banks' hero returns to the real world. It's a necessary journey, in step with an ancient tradition of storytelling.

Fantasy makes frequent appearances in work by many Scottish writers, including Muriel Spark and Ronald Frame. And in his story *Feathered Choristers*, Brian McCabe develops the profoundly disturbing concept that children rather than adults are prone to mental breakdown. McCabe uses fantastic images to introduce concepts which would otherwise be difficult to develop or explain, but which give an extraordinary insight into a young mind on the edge of collapse, a mind which uses fantasy as a comfort, a relief from the miseries of home and school.

Social realism may be the dominant feature of twentieth-century Scottish writing, but the continued attraction of fantasy suggests we need other ways of exploring human behaviour and existence; and to do that, we have to find other worlds to explore, to discover new ways of seeing the obvious.

In *Death in a Nut*, a tale by the traditional storyteller Duncan Williamson, Jack captures and imprisons Death to save his mother, but finds he cannot live himself. He has taken the thing that keeps the world alive.

> Death cam to the door and he ran his hand doon the face o the scythe, he sput on his thumb and he run it up the face o the scythe, an he says tae Jack, 'I see you've sharpened it, Jack, and ye made a good job o it. Well, I hev some people to see in the village. But remember, I'll come back fir yir mother some day, but seein you been guid to me I'll make it a wee while!' An Death walkit away.
>
> From *Death in a Nut* Duncan Williamson

The everyday circumstances of our existence, our social life and the world we inhabit are immaterial to what we find when we embrace the fantastic. At its most basic level, we know or can predict what will happen. But when we step into the unknown we discover something beyond the material, something in which our physical existence plays no part and which it can never touch.

Tartan Myths

Every nicht I used tae hang my troosers up
At the back o the bedroom door.
I rue the day, I must've been a jay,
I'll never hang them there ony more.
For the wife she used to ramble through my pooches
When I was fast asleep beneath the quilt,
And in the morning when I woke
I was always stoney broke,
So that's the reason noo I wear the kilt.
From *Why I Wear the Kilt* Harry Lauder

In October, 1759, James Macpherson met the dramatist John Home on the Moffat bowling green and told him he had translated what he believed were verses of ancient Highland poetry. He had several examples in his possession and, with some reluctance, displayed his wares.

Home was so impressed he passed the poems on to Hugh Blair, who was about to become Professor of Belles Lettres and Rhetoric at Edinburgh University. These early pieces led to a friendship and collaboration between Macpherson and Blair which resulted in *Fragments of Ancient Poetry, Collected in the Highlands of Scotland, and Translated from the Gaelic or Erse Language,* published in 1760. Macpherson claimed his pamphlet contained shards of a great, lost, oral history of Scotland and surrendered himself to fame.

The result was remarkable. *Fragments of Ancient Poetry* caught a mood and kindled hopes that Scotland possessed a body of classical poetry on a par with that of ancient Greece or Rome, something to validate our nationhood and recast the Highlander in a civilised light.

Thirteen years after Culloden, the Highlands were still occupied. Inverness Castle was being built with guns at the ready, a massive military road-building programme was underway and the Highlander was considered threatening, strange and bellicose. While the French philosopher Jean Jacques Rousseau had asserted that the Scottish Highlander and American Indian were perfect examples of the Noble Savage, living in simple, unadorned bliss, a state which should be society's ideal, this couldn't be further from how the Highlander was seen in London. It was hoped Macpherson's work could change this view, restore a measure of our national pride and become an emblem of national identity.

Blair raised money to send Macpherson into The Last Great Wilderness in search of mislaid treasures and he made three trips north in August and October 1760, and again in January 1761, visiting Perthshire, Argyll, Inverness-shire, as well as Skye, Mull, the Uists and Benbecula. The result was *Fingal*, published in December 1762. It detailed, he said, the adventures of the third-century Gaelic warrior poet Ossian, son of Fingal:

Then dismal, roaring, fierce, and deep the gloom of battle rolled along; as mist that is poured on the valley, when storms invade the silent sunshine of heaven. The chief moves before in arms, like an angry ghost before a cloud; when meteors inclose him with fire; and the dark winds are in his hand. Carril, far, on the heath, bids the horn of battle sound. He raises the voice of the song, and pours his soul into the minds of heroes.

From *Fingal* James Macpherson

Fingal was greeted even more rapturously than the *Fragments*. The Edinburgh literati thrilled that their faith in Macpherson had been vindicated, and reviews compared his work to Homer, Virgil and Milton. Versions of *Fingal* were translated, initially into Italian, then into the other major European languages. Napoleon is said to have carried a copy wherever he went and is even credited with trying to write something similar in French.

This resulted in a call for more, a demand Macpherson met in 1763 with *Temora, an Epic in Eight Books*. But cynical outsiders detected a contrivance. It fitted the requirements a little too well and its authenticity was questioned. Doubts had already been raised before publication. Dr Samuel Johnson led the accusations and in 1775 he launched an attack on Macpherson's epics. He was convinced it was a massive fraud, that there was no such thing as Ossianic poetry, or even Gaelic literature. Nothing, after all, had been written in Gaelic.

I believe they never existed in any other form than that which we have seen. The editor, or author, never could shew the original; nor can it be shewn by any other; to revenge reasonable incredulity, by refusing evidence, is a degree of insolence, with which the world is not yet acquainted; and stubborn audacity is the last refuge of guilt. It would be easy to shew it if he had it; but whence could it be had? It is too long to be remembered, and the language formerly had nothing written. He has doubtless inserted names that circulate in popular stories, and may have translated some wandering ballads, if any can be found; and the names and some of the images being recollected, make an inaccurate auditor imagine, by the help of Caledonian bigotry, that he has formerly heard the whole.

From *A Journey to the Western Islands
of Scotland* Samuel Johnson

'A Scotchman must be a very sturdy moralist, who does not love Scotland better than truth,' he added.

And, of course, Johnson would have known the egregious James Boswell had met Macpherson. In his *London Journal 1762–63*, Boswell recorded, 'I breakfasted with Macpherson, the translator of *Fingal*, a man of great genius and an honest Scotch Highlander. It did my heart good to hear the spirit with which he talked.' As well it might, Boswell and Macpherson had a lot in common in terms of upward mobility.

Macpherson was a Highlander, born in Ruthven of Badenoch, Inverness-shire, in 1736. He spoke a little Gaelic, had contact with the oral tradition and was sympathetic to Highland culture. He was a boy living in Inverness when the Jacobite standard was raised at Glenfinnan, and he was well aware of the military occupation and the suppression of Highland culture that came in its wake. After studying at Aberdeen and Edinburgh Universities, he returned to Ruthven where he was in charge of the charity school. He was working as a tutor in Edinburgh when he and a pupil made the trip to Moffat.

Enlightenment philosophers believed reason could overcome the problems of the world and steadily improve the human condition. This hardly matched the reality on their doorstep. Man's reason had produced the emerging Industrial Revolution; already there were polluted rivers and smoke-filled skies. Rousseau had tried to stem the tide by advocating a return to what he believed was the natural condition of our ancestors, an open and benign emotionalism. The cult of the Noble or Primitive Savage was on the rise and Ossian fitted perfectly.

When Macpherson's word was doubted, David Hume suggested he should produce the originals, while other supporters like Henry Mackenzie remained convinced that the poems were a genuine, if fragmentary, translation of a third-century Gaelic epic.

Later research has shown the works were not completely fake. Macpherson used up to fifteen original pieces, but changed the themes and atmosphere to suit eighteenth-century taste. There was a desire to avoid the wave of anti-Scots feeling that followed the Jacobite Rebellion of 1745 and there were many who were only too willing to change their names to something more euphonious, to drop their country habits, manner and accents in the rush towards 'sophistication'.

David Hume rejected the accusation that Scots were backward, and promoted Scottish writing in an attempt to negate the anti-Scottish feeling which was so rife in London. At the time, Tobias Smollett claimed anyone could get published so long as they attacked Scotland. Hume wanted to show we could not only produce works that were at least as good as anything London could come up with, but were possibly better and distinctively Scottish. With this aim, he encouraged John Home, author of *Douglas*, and both were enthusiastic about Ossian, which brought Macpherson fame and the beginnings of a fortune. However, success left Macpherson arrogant, vain and resentful. He was appalled by the criticism he had to endure, and entered government service, worked in Florida, became an MP and was involved in Indian politics. Eventually, he bought an estate in Badenoch, where he died in 1796, the same year as Robert Burns.

After Macpherson's death, Henry Mackenzie was appointed convenor of a committee of the Highland Society of Scotland to investigate the authenticity of the Ossianic poems. Mackenzie was author of *The Man of Feeling*, the book Burns said he prized next to the Bible. As editor of *The Lounger*, Mackenzie hailed Burns as a 'Heaven-taught ploughman' and had encouraged the young Walter Scott, who dedicated *Waverley* to Mackenzie, 'our Scottish Addison'.

The Ossian Report was published in 1805. 'The Committee can with confidence state,' they say immediately, 'that such poetry did exist, that it was common, general and in great abundance; that it was of a most impressive and striking sort, in a high degree eloquent, tender and sublime.'

The Committee concludes that Macpherson had added passages of his own to create the epics, especially *Temora*, and that 'a man of a sanguine and somewhat confident disposition like Macpherson is apt to give a degree of carelessness and presumption, that would rather command than conciliate the public suffrage and, in the security of the world's applause, neglects the best means of obtaining it.'

By now Scotland was seen as a nation of Dark Age poetic heroes and innocent tribesmen. Thomas Pennant came north in 1769 and the three-volume account of his adventures inspired travellers for almost half a century. Weather prevented Pennant landing on Staffa, so he published Sir Joseph Banks' description of Fingal's Cave: 'Compared to this, what are the cathedrals or the palaces built by men! Mere models or playthings, imitations as diminutive as his works will always be when compared to those of nature.' Banks, a one-time companion to Captain Cook, 'discovered' the island in 1772 while returning from a voyage to Iceland. The cave, he reckoned, surpassed both the Louvre and St Peter's in Rome.

This gushing description inspired Barthelemy Faujas de Saint Fond to visit the Hebrides and when he reached Dalmally in the autumn of 1784 MacNab the blacksmith's brother could not only recite the verses of Ossian for the Faujas' party, but promised to tell them some curious things about the great poet. Three days later, while lost on the road to Oban, they sheltered by a waterfall, where one of the party, an American, William Thornton, reminded them they were in Fingal's country and the place where they stood had been trodden by the feet of Ossian.

'Scarcely had he uttered these words in a tone of enthusiasm, when an old man, with bare head and white hair, dressed in a flowing drapery of the same colour appeared to us. "It is Ossian!" cried Thornton, "it is that divine poet himself who hastens to us at the mention of the name of his illustrious father. Let us fall at his feet." But the ghost, without uttering a word, without casting a single look towards us, stalked gravely towards the torrent and disappeared.'

Days later they reached their objective. After waiting at Torloisk on Mull they were told at four o'clock on the fourth day that the weather looked promising. The boatmen sang as they rowed to Staffa, because, Faujas reckoned, 'they love everything that reminds them of Ossian, as they seem to regard it as a happiness and honour to conduct strangers to Fingal's Cave'.

He describes the place and its dimensions in some detail – 'I have never found anything which comes near this . . . or can be compared to it' – unaware that the association with Fingal was a blunder perpetrated by Sir Joseph Banks. Its Gaelic name was *an-*

ua-vine, the melodious cave, which Banks transcribed as *an-ua-Fine*, the cave of Fingal.

Jorge Luis Borges said Macpherson had sacrificed honesty to the greater glory of Scotland and thereby wrote the 'first Romantic poem in European literature'. Travellers followed Pennant and Faujas to emote passages by heart at fearsome waterfalls. And the lie was given substance in places like The Hermitage, outside Dunkeld, temples designed in the Ossian manner. Ossian Stones or sites associated with Fingal were discovered nationwide, seldom far from a centre of population.

James Oswald, the leading Scottish composer of the day, set some Ossian poems to music, as did Schubert and Brahms. And in Germany, where Ossian was especially popular, operas were based on his works. Goethe uses the Ossian poems, along with the works of Homer, in his novel *The Sorrows of Young Werther* and compared Macpherson to Shakespeare. Ossian was said to have comforted Napoleon on St Helena and his imperial apartments in Paris and Rome were decorated with Ossianic scenes, including the bard welcoming the ghosts of Napoleon's soldiers.

The art historian Murdo Macdonald believes that Macpherson began a Celtic revival which found its most developed expression over a century later in the Glasgow of Charles Rennie Mackintosh and the Edinburgh of Patrick Geddes. The painter Alexander Runciman taught Henry Raeburn and Alexander Nasmyth, and used scenes from Ossian as the main features of his murals for Penicuik House.

The poems were published at a time when Highland culture was being systematically shattered, when there were punitive moves to replace it with something more suitable. The 1747 Proscription Act, that specifically banned the wearing of tartan and Highland dress in the Highlands by any but the burgeoning Highland regiments, was still in force. Between Culloden and Waterloo over 100 battalions were raised in the North and by the time His Majesty King George IV appeared in Edinburgh in kilt and tights in 1822, the military associations were obvious. This was one of a number of measures aimed at destroying the clan system and disrupting Highland life to weaken social cohesion and prevent another uprising.

Macpherson paved the way for Scotland's perpetual Noble Savage, Robert Burns, who, in turn, inspired a barbarous successor, James Hogg. Burns himself had nurtured the myth of the peasant poet. In his Preface to the Kilmarnock edition, he 'begs his readers, particularly the Learned and the Polite, who may honour him with a perusal, that they will make every allowance for Education and Circumstances of Life.'

Which is barely a step from Henry Mackenzie's 'Heaven-taught ploughman'. And while he did what he could to confound easy analysis, the least that can be said is that Burns was a widely read, intelligent, sophisticated writer whose influence on Scottish life and literature was total, especially on the man who picked up where he left off, as a collector of traditional songs.

Sir Walter Scott's position is at least as complicated as Burns' or Hogg's though he has suffered more from our desire to reduce our writers to a single dimension, to see them not as they were, as complete, contradictory individuals, but to find them in easily digested pieces. Burns is the perpetual hero, Hogg the misunderstood fool and Scott the perpetual villain.

Burns, Hogg and Scott played along with and to some extent helped create their own stereotypes and there are similarities in the ways in which they allowed whimsy to overtake the realities of their existence.

'This open-hearted and sensible man lived partly in a world of fantasy. His business dealings are almost incomprehensible, and suggest that he never really wanted to know how things stood. His imagination was out of kilter with the facts; his finances represent a degree of optimism not far short of the manic. He knew himself very well, but could not have said whence his deepest and truest strokes came,' says Allan Massie of Scott. Something similar could also be said of Burns and Hogg.

Scott was middle-class before the term was invented. A Scottish patriot and Unionist, the son of a successful lawyer, he was educated at Edinburgh High School and University, was apprenticed to his father, became an advocate and for more than thirty years was Sheriff of Selkirkshire; he was Principal Clerk to the Court of Session for almost twenty-five years. On both sides he was descended from the oldest Border families.

A childhood bout of infantile paralysis left him lame in one leg. He lived till the age of eight at his grandfather's farm at Sandy-knowe, near Kelso, beside Smailholm Tower, which Robert Scott also owned. Smailholm left a big impression:

> And ever by the winter's hearth,
> Old tales I heard of woe or mirth,
> Of lovers' sleights, of ladies charms,
> Of witches' spells, of warriors' arms:
> Of patriot battles won of old
> By Wallace wight and Bruce the bold;
> Of later fields of feud and flight,
> When pouring from the Highland height,
> The Scottish clans, in headlong sway,
> Had swept the scarlet ranks away.
> While stretched at length upon the floor,
> Again I fought each combat o'er,
> Pebbles and shells in order laid,
> The mimic ranks of war displayed;
> And onward still the Scottish Lion bore,
> And still the scattered Southron fled before
>> From *Marmion*, Introduction,
>> Canto III Sir Walter Scott

He was captivated by the romanticism of Ossian and could 'repeat without remorse whole cantos'. As a writer, Scott evolved from ballad collector to ballad editor and imitator to a writer of narrative poems which drew on ballad techniques and themes:

Where gleaming with the setting sun,
One burnish'd sheet of living gold,
Loch Katrine lay beneath him rolld,
In all her length far winding lay,
With promontory, creek and bay,
And islands that empurpled bright,
Floated amid the livelier light,
And mountains that like giants stand,
To sentinel enchanted land,
High on the south huge Ben Venue,
Down on the lake in masses threw,
Crags, knolls and mounds, confusedly hurled,
The fragments of an earlier world

From *The Lady of the Lake* Sir Walter Scott

Scott made his name with *The Lady of the Lake*, published in 1810. A year later it had sold more than 20,000 copies. Thousands came to see for themselves and to witness the birth of the Highlands as spectacle.

The Lady of the Lake signalled Scott's breakthrough as a writer. 'I concluded that I had at last fixed a nail in the proverbial inconsistent wheel of fortune,' he wrote at the time.

Earlier narrative poems such as *The Lay of the Last Minstrel* (1805) and *Marmion* (1808) combined patriotic sentiments and Unionist feelings, featuring sections which appealed to the rising vogue for recitation, raised the spirit and carried the poem beyond the plains where Scott sought to instruct or inform:

O Caledonia! Stern and wild,
Meet nurse for a poetic child!
Land of brown heath and shaggy wood,
Land of the mountain and the flood,
Land of my sires, what mortal hand
Can e'er untie the filial band,
That knits me to thy rugged strand!

From *The Lay of the
Last Minstrel* Sir Walter Scott

Before 1810, Loch Katrine and the surrounding hills were un-known and virtually inaccessible. Scott himself made the claim that the only way to access the area from the Trossachs was by using 'a sort of ladder, composed of the branches and roots of the trees'. After 1810 thousands came to view this wild spot. As one commentator noted, 'It is a well ascertained fact that from the date of publication the post horse duty in Scotland rose in an extra-ordinary degree, from which it may be perceived that sometimes poetry has a solid value even from the point of view of the publican and tax gatherer.'

Scott boosted the tourist industry that Macpherson had in-itiated. By the 1820s John Knox's painting *Landscape with Tourists at Loch Katrine* presented a visual response to *The Lady of the Lake*. The key elements are in place – scenic grandeur, rural pastimes such as fishing, and a piper. The view is tranquil. Every hint of warlike restlessness has been purged from the landscape. Here are pliant, agreeable people in a peaceful place where tourists are welcome.

When his friend Lord George Byron created his own publishing sensation in 1812 with the first two cantos of *Childe Harold's Pilgrimage*, Scott decided his future lay as a novelist. 'Byron beat me,' he said, realising his vogue was over, and, at the age of forty-three, he began a new career.

Jane Porter's *The Scottish Chiefs* had been published in the same year as *The Lady of the Lake*. It was one of the most successful novels of the nineteenth century, running to many editions and inspiring a catalogue of imitators. She had doubtless been stimu-lated by Scott's poetry, and Scott may have unconsciously repaid the compliment. His first work of fiction was *Waverley*, published in 1814.

It was at that instant, that, looking around him, he saw the wild dress and appearance of his Highland associates, heard their whispers in an uncouth and unknown language, looked upon his own dress, so unlike that which he had worn from his infancy, and wished to awake from what seemed at the moment a dream, strange and horrible and unnatural. 'Good God!' he muttered, 'Am I then a traitor to my country, a renegade to my standard, and a foe, as that poor dying wretch expressed himself, to my native England?'

From Waverley Sir Walter Scott

Edward Waverley gets lost in the excitement of the Highland Dream. The primitive and the picturesque collide, and in Flora MacIvor he meets the epitome of Romantic Scotland

Her brother, Fergus, a Highland chief, introduces Captain Waverley as 'a worshiper of the Celtic muse'. Discussing the role of the bard, Flora tells Waverley, 'The recitation of poems recording the feats of heroes, the complaints of lovers, and the wars of contending tribes, forms the chief amusement of a winter fireside in the Highlands. Some of these are said to be very ancient, and if they are ever translated into any of the languages of civilised Europe, cannot fail to produce a deep and general sensation.'

Waverley is shown one of Flora's favourite haunts, where in an enchanted glen, gazing at a waterfall and playing a small Scottish harp, she induces in Waverley a feeling of romantic delight that is almost painful, making him want to leave, to be alone 'that he might decipher and examine at leisure the complication of emotions which now agitated his bosom . . . A few irregular strains introduced a prelude of a wild and peculiar tone, which harmonized well with the distant waterfall, and the soft sigh of the evening breeze in the rustling leaves of an aspen which overhung the seat of the fair harpress.'

The novel was hugely successful. Jane Austen quipped, 'Walter Scott has no business to write novels, especially good ones – it is not fair. He has fame and profit enough as a poet and should not be taking the bread out of other people's mouths. I do not mean to like *Waverley* if I can help it – but I fear I must.'

The novel is set during the Jacobite Rebellion. Scott hoped to create a new mythology for Scotland, new narratives of Scottish history and culture which could forgive the internecine past and allow post-Union Scotland to come to terms with its equal partnership with England. He was aware of the damage of rebellions, religious strife and the age-old feud with the English, and resolved that the past must be changed and a certain dignity introduced into the story.

Scott is the first example of a world bestseller. He created the modern novel and though his achievements have been superseded, his revolutionary use of history and landscape, psychology and romance, suggest a deeper purpose than simple entertainment or a delight in the well told tale. His influence on world literature was enormous; he inspired Pushkin, Gogol and Balzac, and influenced Fenimore Cooper, the Brontës and Dickens.

His position as a novelist became muddied when he gave his romantic inclinations substance. In August 1822, Scotland was blessed with a visit from King George IV, the first by a reigning monarch in almost 200 years. The event was accompanied by all the pomp and ceremony that Scott could discover or devise. Acting as pageant master, Scott invented a mythology of Highland customs and dress which were, and still are, accepted as ancient tradition. He was responsible for arranging everything 'from the ordering of a procession, to the cut of a button and the embroidering of a cross'.

His Majesty came north regaled in Royal Stewart tartan and pink, flesh-coloured tights. The royal visit led to the kilt being adopted as national dress. Edinburgh Castle was refurbished, the Scottish Crown Jewels were rediscovered and displayed. Highlanders and their ancient traditions, dances and even Highland Games, all adapted or invented by Scott, were given a prominent role in the ceremonies.

Scott's son-in-law and biographer John Gibson Lockhart dubbed the process Celtification, a 'plaided panorama' and grumbled, 'Scott has ridiculously made us appear to be a nation of Highlanders, and the bagpipe and the tartan are the order of the day.'

Traditions clearly had to be invented. There were no precedents for such occasions. But while this was going on there was a different reality in Scotland. Many Highland communities had been cleared. Others had emigrated, were absorbed into Lowland anonymity, or had been conscripted and forced into service. The Highlands were no longer threatening. They had been reinvented as a setting for romance and adventure, which was accompanied by a rise in antiquarianism and lore. Societies devoted to preserving Highland dress and pageantry were created, allowing the Highlander in his new role to be admired as a spectacle.

Scott's influence was so powerful it affected virtually every strand of Scottish life. Having promoted Scotland as an international tourist attraction, the place he referred to as 'conundrum castle', his home at Abbotsford, became an important part of the tourist circuit, as did Scott himself, with a stream of visitors arriving to meet the great man, or simply be in his presence.

With the construction of Abbotsford Scott played a decisive role in setting down the national qualities of Scottish architecture, and had an enormous influence on what was to become known as Scottish baronial architecture. In 1844 Fox Talbot photographed the house for what was the second photographic book ever published, *Sun Pictures in Scotland*.

The Heart of Midlothian is the basis of an opera by Hamish McCunn, the Greenock-born composer better known for *The Land of the Mountain and the Flood*, which was also borrowed from Scott; and other novels provided the plots for many European operas such as *Lucia di Lammermuir* and *The Fair Maid of Perth*.

Nor did the painter John Knox give the only response to *The Lady of the Lake*. Horatio McCulloch was a pupil of Knox and his grand landscapes such as *Glencoe* and *Loch Maree* preceded the postcard image of the Highlands by distancing the Highlander and the landscape. They provided a template of Highland painting for the Victorian age, showing a landscape without people. This is a wilderness where the only living creatures are deer or cattle, which is an interesting transition: sheep had previously symbolised Arcadian landscapes.

And the spirit of Scott inhabits other nineteenth-century Scottish paintings, either in the direct illustration of scenes from his works, or in interpretations of his sense of romance, history, social discourse or commentary.

Following the death of Scott and the loss of both Hogg and Galt, Scottish literature came under the influence of Professor John Wilson, Hogg's *Blackwood's* ridiculer and tease, whose novels celebrated an intelligent, pious peasantry progressing from squalor and tribulation to an innocent earthly paradise. Wilson used his editorial role at *Blackwood's Magazine* to promote idyllic, parochial simplicity.

The burgeoning industries needed a literate and numerate working class. Publications appeared which catered to this class and formed their tastes. For the most part, broadsheets and chapbooks had long been the most popular source of written entertainment; cheaply printed publications full of saucy tales, naughty poems and reworkings of popular songs. The Kirk took a dim view of the reading habits of the urban poor and deliberate attempts were made to elevate their taste.

A Glasgow publisher supplied this material in the form of David Robertson's *Whistle-Binkie*, bringing stability and couthiness to every home.

The *Whistle-Binkie* collections did not represent the only kind of writing, nor the only writers working, in Scotland from 1832 to 1890 but they were extremely popular and presented a cosmetic view of Scottish life and values in a rural escapist literature that ignored or distorted the social and political realities of the Highland Clearances and massive urbanisation.

They were certainly influenced by and could even be said to have risen, fully formed, from the writings and teaching of Professor John Wilson, whose work did much to establish a head in-the-sand ruralism. Domestic values were enhanced and religious life and teachings were seen as the basis of decency. Morality was preserved at all costs and the status quo maintained. The *Whistle-Binkie* anthologists and the Kailyard movement shared many aspects.

The Kailyard exploited a series of constants. Locality has given Scottish literature an identity, rhythm and voice it would otherwise lack. It has consistently thrown up a number of writers whose work rejoices in the accents, mannerisms and geography of place. It is difficult to imagine the work of these writers being set in another country, in another part of the British Isles, or even in another part of Scotland.

The Kailyarders exported Scottish virtues abroad and simultaneously reinforced them at home, where their main weapon was an immediately recognisable voice, which chimed with the popular movements of the times. An international audience was clearly taken by the freshness, the flattery and the innocent harmless fun; after all a Scots village would clearly be inhabited by ridiculous, faintly gormless folk with silly names. This view was underlined by *Punch* cartoons, mostly by Scots, which emphasised the Kailyard virtues while popularising the image of dourness and stinginess abroad.

And while all this was going on, Sir Harry Lauder was treading the boards. His role in spreading the tartan myth can neither be under-estimated nor over-stated. Initial success in Scotland and England led to twenty-two American tours. 'The superior person will perhaps sniff if I suggest that no man since Sir Walter Scott has warmed the world's heart to Scotland more surely than Sir Harry Lauder. His genius is a thing apart,' wrote H.V. Morton.

The Kailyard novels by S.R. Crocket, John Watson and J.M. Barrie painted a sanitised, emulsified picture of rural sentimentality. These scenes from a manse window at best ignored the iniquities of what was happening around them, and at worst deliberately strove to disguise them.

The term 'Kailyard', which literally means 'cabbage patch' describes a school of rural sentimentality, mostly published in

Christian magazines. The essential ingredients revolved around timeless, isolated rural communities peopled with characters who represented solid virtues: the minister who voices pastoral morality; the industrious son who rises by dint of hard work; and the honest tenant farmers who give of their best for their families' improvement.

Kailyard writers exploited the parochial; there were no balancing virtues. Life was monotonous; black and white. There were no grey areas. Everyone knew their place. Changes of heart, especially before death, were common. Family reunions and sudden conversions shifted plots entirely.

Behind these well-to-do folks lay a stock of rapacious landlords and self-satisfied incomers, who were usually victims of petty presumptions which were earnestly revealed and kindly forgiven, assuming the miscreant had learned a lesson. These characters inhabited a well-defined arcadia of village life, far removed from the realities of nineteenth-century Scotland, its industrial development, poverty and high mortality rate. The dramas revolved around the minister or the dominie, often the same person, and the standard village communal events such as weddings and funerals, strangers arriving and familiar departures. The city appeared as a distant place to which people disappeared.

Robert Kirk, Carsethorn, had a packet of peppermint lozenges in the crown of his 'lum' hat – deponed to by Elizabeth Douglas or Barr, in Barnbogrie, whose husband, Weelum Barr, put on the hat of the aforesaid Robert Kirk by mistake for his own, whereupon the peppermints fell to the floor and rolled under the pews in most unseemly fashion. Elizabeth Kirk is of the opinion that this should be brought to the notice of Session, she herself always taking her peppermint while genteelly wiping her mouth with the corner of handkerchief.

From *The Stickit Minister* S.R. Crockett

Foremost among the champions of the Kailyard, was the founder and editor of *British Weekly,* William Robertson Nicoll. A son of the manse, born and educated in the north-east of Scotland, Nicoll trained as a Free Church minister before moving to London where he established a career with Hodder & Stoughton, one of the Kailyard's leading publishers. *British Weekly* and the *Christian Leader,* a Baptist weekly published in Glasgow, were especially responsive to Kailyard fiction.

Hugh C. Rae is particularly clear about the Free Kirk's role: 'As always with the Free Church it endeavoured to control what was actually being disseminated into the culture as a whole. Naturally, they were very much in favour of a stable, over-sentimentalised comfortable sort of society, a society in which they could exist without ever in any way obviously being seen as repressive.'

Nicoll was ruled by the principles of publishing economics which determined, then as now, that a successful story theme be exploited to its utmost. He was also inclined to support his fellow Scots, particularly if they signed up to Free Church Associations. He encouraged Ian Maclaren to take up writing and championed the young J.M. Barrie, whose early magazine sketches of Scotch life were so popular he was encouraged to bring them together as a book.

Tammy Mealmaker the wright, pronounced wir-icht . . . who died a bachelor, had been soured in his youth by a disappointment in love, of which he spoke but seldom.

She lived far away in a town where he had wandered in the days when his blood ran hot, and they became engaged. Unfortunately, however, Tammy forgot her name, and he never knew the address; so there the affair ended, to his silent grief.

From *Auld Licht Idylls* J.M. Barrie

Barrie's mother, Margaret Ogilvy, belonged to a puritanical sect, the Auld Lichts, for whom the Sabbath began at 6 p.m. on

Saturday. They objected to hymns, written prayers and sermons, and their precentors had to deliver the whole of the psalm rather than the opening line.

Auld Licht Idylls was a collection of twelve stories Barrie claimed were based on his mother's fireside tales. They were published in 1888 and a second collection, *A Window in Thrums*, was published the following year.

James Robertson feels one shouldn't make the mistake of thinking that everything about the Kailyard is bad, quoting the fact that they helped to preserve the use of Scots language in literature. 'I've recently read Barrie's novel *The Little Minister* which would certainly qualify as a "Kailyard" novel,' he says, 'and it's witty, it's funny, the plot's well constructed, and it also verges into that area of fantasy mixing with reality, so it's not altogether bad. But it's got nowhere to go.'

Andrew O'Hagan reckons the Kailyard has had considerable influence, something that would horrify contemporary writers: 'There is more domestic interior in Scottish writing today than there is of grand pageant.'

The single vision of the Kailyard meant urban fiction was isolated and truthful, and real life depictions of Highland or rural life were suppressed. In particular, Gaelic culture was overlooked. The Kailyard dream got a rude awakening when *The House with the Green Shutters* by George Douglas Brown was published in 1901. But it was a single blow and, soon after writing it, Brown died of pneumonia.

John Macdougall Hay's 1914 novel *Gillespie* is similarly unrelenting. It also traces the fall of a self-made tyrant whose life ends in death and destruction. Hay targeted what he saw as a rising tide of materialism, and while he had clearly read Brown, his sense of predestiny and evil carried echoes of Hogg.

Gillespie Strang is a demonic force and though he has a sense of greatness and through his herring curing business carries the vision of a future for the Highlands, his overwhelming greed destroys everything around him. Hay modelled Barbie on his home town of Tarbert and he used the Highland setting as more than a backdrop for romance and mysticism, though his writing does display highly developed extravagant richness and concentration on detail, especially in his descriptions of the natural world such as sea and light and the beauty of the fish.

Both Brown and Hay carry echoes of Stevenson, especially the later books such as *Master of Ballantrae* and *Weir of Hermiston*. And Hay's friend, Neil Munro, similarly used the Highlands as a setting for *John Splendid* and *The New Road*, which are cast in the *Kidnapped* model. Munro's *Para Handy* tales, with their set cast of characters, sly humour and small town settings up and down the West Coast of Scotland present a warmer view of Highland life.

The Nationalist movement of the 1930s brought a small tartan explosion, especially in the works of D.K. Broster which both encouraged and exploited the tartan mythology. And even though the novels of Neil Gunn and later Iain Crichton Smith portrayed a realistic picture of Highland life, they barely frayed the edges of the tartan myth.

Compton Mackenzie's 'finely observed comedy of Scottish life and manners' *Monarch of the Glen*, was originally published in 1941 and appealed to an audience who expected a Scotland of dependable emotions and romance.

Just as Scott had been inspired by Ossian, Mackenzie's inspiration came from a boyhood reading of Sir Walter Scott. At the age of eight he was given a copy of Scott's *Tales of a Grandfather* and soon after 'travelled northward alone. It was near dusk on an evening in earliest Spring. Somebody in the railway-carriage announced that we were crossing the border, and I craned my head out of the window to enjoy the magical sensation. Down the long train came a faint sound of cheering and from windows far ahead I could see hats being waved. An austere landscape in the fast-fading dusk, a stream of flamy smoke from the engine, a few cheers ringing above the roar of the train, a few hats waving; not much perhaps, but enough for a child of eight to sit back again in a dim railway-carriage and dream over, his heart blazoned like a herald's tabard with the bright symbols of his country's life, his heart draped like a hatchment with the sombre memories of defeat after defeat. Thence onwards I lived secretly in the past of my country.'

Born Edward Montague Compton in Hartlepool in 1883, he reinstated the Mackenzie lineage to his surname as his emotional links with Scotland grew. Mackenzie settled in Scotland when he was forty-five and for a long time he was Scotland's best-known writer, a position maintained by his regular appearance on the front page of national newspapers in a series of whisky advertisements, coupled with an ability to offer instant opinions on the issues of the day.

He sprang from a famous theatrical family: his father was an actor-manager and his sister was a well-known actress. He was educated in England and his early reputation was as an English novelist, yet he was a founder member of the Scottish National Party and his popular reputation rests on a series of Highland comedies which portray Scotland as a playground of bumbling land-owners and half-witted Highlanders.

Mackenzie had a successful career as a novelist before coming to Scotland. Admirers of his early works include Henry James who in the *Times Literary Supplement* in 1914 crowned him 'very much the greatest talent of a new generation'. He was friendly with D.H. Lawrence and his novel *Sinister Street*, a book Henry James said 'emancipated the English novel' was banned by W.H. Smith's lending library, but enjoyed great success in America, where it influenced the young Scott Fitzgerald.

In 1928 he came to Scotland and settled on Barra. His first foray into the Scottish character is in *The Four Winds of Love*, published in four parts between 1937 and 1945.

The greatest paradox of Mackenzie's life is that his earlier works and later exhaustive autobiographical volumes have been overtaken in the popular imagination by works which have diminished his reputation. A series of novels set in the Highlands such as *Hunting the Fairies, Monarch of the Glen, The Rival Monster* and

Whisky Galore! rewove the tartan myth internationally and bequeathed Scotland with some of the most internationally recognisable and enduring images of the twentieth century. Of these, *Monarch of the Glen* (1941) and *Whisky Galore!* (1947) are the best known: the first because of a recent television series which is loosely based on the novel, and the second through Alexander Mackendrick's wonderful film, which spawned a series of stylistic sequels such as *The Maggie*, *The Bridal Path* and *Geordie* among others, all of which underlined the fact that comic films about Scotland were good for the box office.

It was the custom of Glenbogle for Angus MacQuat or another of the pipers to rouse Ben Nevis every morning at eight by playing beneath his window the ancient *Iomradh Mhic 'ic Eachainn* or *Fame of Mac 'ic Eachainn*, in which the virtue, nobility, valour and generosity of the Chieftain of Ben Nevis were celebrated with what the less imaginative Southerner might have thought a certain amount of exaggeration. The tune, however, had a fine lilt and possessed a persuasive drive to energetic action which the shrilling of an alarm clock lacks. Even the guest who had not been warned about the significance of this aubade often sprang out of bed to look out of the window and see what was being killed.

From *Monarch of the Glen* Compton Mackenzie

Mackenzie's novels became hugely popular at home as well as becoming one of our best exports. There's no doubt they appealed to an audience who expected a reliable Scotland of emotion and romance, and for whom the added component of the Highlander's ability to laugh at himself was warmly welcomed. It would be comforting to think that this humour was not directed at Scotland in general or the Highlander in particular, but at national stereotypes. If this was Mackenzie's intention, he failed; unfortunately he perpetuated the myth.

And while the tartan myths have obscured some of our greatest writers, they have opened a market for others, not always Scots. American visitors flock to bookshops in search of the latest tartan bodice-ripper from Diana Gabaldon whose *Outlander* series of novels contains a handy glossary of exotic Scottish phrases. Gabaldon's books are rampant bestsellers across the States and she is clearly delivering what her market expects from a Scottish novel. She and her family are based in Arizona.

She chose eighteenth-century Scotland after watching a *Doctor Who* episode 'with a cute little Scottish character'. 'If you really want to write a book, it doesn't really matter where you set it. The important thing is you should just pick a place. So I began with no outline, no plot, no characters; nothing but a time and a place. But I knew the important thing was to write.'

How in the name of God did this happen? I asked myself some time later. Six weeks ago I had been innocently collecting wild flowers on a Scottish hill, to take home to my husband. I was now shut in the room of a rural inn, awaiting a completely different husband, whom I scarcely knew, with firm orders to consummate a forced marriage, at risk of my life and liberty.

And what about my old husband? My stomach knotted with grief and fear. What would Frank be thinking now? What would he be feeling? I had been gone for more than a month; he would have been searching for me, calling out the police as his concern turned to fear, turning the Scottish countryside upside down. Not far enough, though; it would never occur to him to look inside a fairies' hill, even were such a thing possible.

From *Cross Stitch* Diana Gabaldon

Cross Stitch is not part of the *Outlander* series: Stonehenge features as a sort of time machine and there's an encounter with the Loch Ness Monster.

Gabaldon has written an Introduction to an American edition of *Ivanhoe* and she is one of a number of writers whose grasp of tartan reality is greater than our own. These books form a genre called time travel romances. Many of these stories rely on the predictable primary school ending: 'I woke up and it was all a dream.' Except, here it only seems like a dream. Middle-class American women, having a restful yet romantically stimulating holiday, travel back to a time of romance and mystery. Karen Marie Moning's titles give you a flavour: *The Dark Highlander, Kiss of the Highlander,* and *The Highlander's Touch.*

While on Mull, I came across a hardback copy of *Legend of the Celtic Stone* by Michael Phillips, subtitled *An Epic Saga of Scotland and her People.*

It is the first in a series of novels called *Caledonia,* and was left in Mull by a Canadian who had come on a pilgrimage to Scotland as a result of reading it. She was visiting some of the places mentioned in the book; Edinburgh, Glencoe and Iona being the most significant. The novel's publishers call themselves 'The Leaders in Christian Fiction!' The visitor had left it in the hope it would inspire others as it had inspired her.

Michael Phillips ends his Introduction: 'When Scotland's magic begins to weave its spell, you will likely discover that it has affected you with the sense that there may be Scots blood in your *own* veins – or at least that this pilgrimage in search of heritage and roots is one every one of us shares. This, therefore, is *your* quest as well . . . because, in a sense, wherever you call home, Scotland is your land as well.

'Truly the account of Caledonia *is* every man and every woman's story . . . for in a mysterious and magical sense – and perhaps more in fact than we are aware – *we are all Scots together.'*

This view isn't something contemporary Scottish writers would welcome. Many feel the tartan myth is irrelevant. It fuels our tourist industry but has little place in a multi-cultural Scotland.

'It is designed mainly for overseas consumption,' says Irvine Welsh. 'It is designed to pull tourists in, to make the diaspora feel good about where they come from; it's also swallowed up by people at home, particularly people who aren't doing so well. They often find these myths quite empowering, after eighteen pints before the bell goes.'

Even if the tartan myths embarrass us, it's unfair to criticise our writers for inventing them; after all myth-making and making up stories is what writers do, have always done and are still doing. And our mythology is not confined to plaided panoramas or an imagined egalitarian kingdom.

Irvine Welsh admits: 'There are all different kinds of constructions of Scotland. My construction is in some ways just as false as the Walter Scott construction. I don't try to paint any sort of accurate picture of what I see as a novelist. What I'm trying to do is give myself licence to talk about the bigger truths I feel are being ignored.

'I'm probably operating in the very same way,' he says, 'but in a radical rather than reactionary way, using all these novelists' tools and techniques to try to get to a broader truth, rather than as a form of artifice.'

Which would appear to be part of a writer's job description; though it's rare to find their fictions becoming a nation's reality, and rarer still to see them multiplied out of recognition in a country with an identity crisis of its own.

An obvious negative effect of the tartan myth has been to suppress true Highland identity and, in particular, Gaelic culture. While the Edinburgh literati were swooning over Ossian, one of the finest Gaelic poets, Duncan ban Macintyre was a member of the City Guard; and when Johnson railed against the verse, Robert Fergusson was celebrating Edinburgh's High Street, at that time an area well beyond the literati's ken.

Highlanders may have embraced their new identity, but the influence of writers like Sorley MacLean and Iain Crichton Smith have led Gaelic and Highland-based writers to import realism. And while our national focus on the tartan myth has promulgated a one-dimensional view of the country and ourselves, this, in turn, has led to a disregard of urban culture. Recent writing and the international success of films such as *Trainspotting*, which humorously portrays a Highland environment as actively hostile, and television series such as Ian Rankin's *Rebus* and the Taggart tales, may have helped to turn the tide; for it does appear that others are beginning to adjust their view of Scotland. Maybe more than us, they seem able to accept that fantasy and reality can coexist perfectly well. The downside could be that, given the examples mentioned and Irvine Welsh's own admission, we may find ourselves with a psychopathic junkie or a soor-faced polisman as alternative Ossians.

Hell on Earth

It's so much easier now.
Once, it was blood
The stricken
Yell of the victim
And the horrible, holy, sticky hands of the priest.

But now, just press the button
The god comes down at once
Clean, prompt and deferential
As electricity
Not even inquiring
What it is we want to destroy.
Comparative Religion Elma Mitchell

Scotland's religious membership is in decline. As congregations
drop, buildings built for worship turn into pubs, nightclubs and
the like. Or they're left to rot, preserved as architectural relics.

Yet, anyone who has been in Glasgow during an Old Firm
match can testify that religion still tears our country apart.
Every time there's a sectarian murder we are told the trouble
comes from a minority of bigots. But still the songs ring out.
At its most visible, the bigotry is played out on the Old Firm
terraces, but the infection runs deep, mainly across west
Central Scotland, covering generations in communities split
by prejudice and boundaries marked by late-night violence and
graffiti.

In 2001 the Scottish Parliament introduced a Bill to combat
what it called sectarianism and religious hatred; its very existence
suggests no single factor has influenced our psyche more than our

relationship with God and the belief of others in what they see as the worthiness of His cause.

Scottish writing has been shaped, and, in many cases, twisted by faith; and this religious sensibility has formed our way of looking at the world, producing a literature that is distinctly Scottish. It's difficult to say if this darkness evolved or was always present; but thriller writer Muriel Gray, for one, doesn't doubt its existence.

'There's definitely a darkness at the heart of Scottish literature,' she says, 'and it's hard to say whether it comes from geography, climate, religious history or the Scottish character. But there's no denying it.'

Nothing is more important to literature than imagination. And Scottish writers have had a stormy relationship with those who would restrict or control their thoughts, which comes down to an interpretation of faith and how we've expressed it. In early times our writers' imaginations soared with divine inspiration. But since the Reformation, literary flights of fancy have been darkened by Calvinism.

Literature and religion share an understanding of fundamental truths about who we are and our place in the universe. Both offer explanation and analysis. Both interpret the world around us. So it's not surprising that in ancient times, writing was considered a sacred act and words were seen as vehicles of divine truth.

Fifteen hundred years ago, Irish monks brought us literacy and the Word of God. The sacred Word was painstakingly decorated with gold and coloured inks and bound in calf-hide, books which formed the heart of Scotland's first known written culture. The surviving manuscripts reveal a sense of wonder in the men who wrote them. For the early Celtic monks, heaven wasn't a remote concept, something indefinable or obscure. It touched our world and God's presence could be felt everywhere.

'They were out to give their own expression of the Word,' says Kenneth White. 'The Word was God, certainly, but Columba is going to give his Columban version of the Word, and so the Word is gradually mixed up with wind, sea, snow, birds and that's where Celtic Christianity evolves its own thought and its own poetics which is, in my opinion, very, very beautiful.'

Robert Crawford agrees: 'If you think of what I would see as a great foundation stone of Scottish poetry, the *Altus Prosator*, often attributed to St Columba, it's a poem with whirlpools in it, with exciting landscapes and seascapes and it wants to take in everything. It's almost structured like a great cathedral, but it's a cathedral of language and it's bonding the world as written down by monks to the Word, the Logos, the Word of God.'

Irrigating clouds showering wet winter from sea fountains
from floods of the abysses three-fourths down through fishes
up to the skyey purlieus in deep blue whirlpools
good rain for cornfields vineyard-bloom and grain-yields
driven by blasts emerging from their airy treasuring
desiccating not the land-marches but the facing sea-marshes.
From *Altus Prosator*, St Columba, trans. Edwin Morgan

Altus Prosator (The Maker on High) is the earliest known Scottish poem. There is no proof that Columba is the author, but it was ascribed to him at an early date. He is known to have written hymns which were sung in Iona and modern scholars are certain the attribution is correct. The poem was well known and admired and copies exist in Britain and Ireland as well as on the Continent. Its message of hope and faith can be felt today.

'For Columba, God is God, and the ministry of Jesus and the comfort of the Holy Ghost are firmly maginalised,' says Edwin Morgan. 'Without being unorthodox, the poem is a concentrated, relentless blast of fearful praise for the *Altus Prosator* of the opening line, and, friends, you better believe it.'

And on Judgement Day, in Morgan's translation:

Standing in fear and trembling with divine judgement
    assembling
We shall stammer what we expended before life was ended
    Faced by rolling videos of our crimes . . .

It used to be thought Scottish literature began in the late Middle Ages with poets such as Robert Henryson, William Dunbar and Gavin Douglas, but the discovery of poems such as *Altus Prosator* and others in Gaelic, Norse, Latin, Welsh, Old English and Scots, written by Scots or by poets living in Scotland, has caused the date to be adjusted by almost a thousand years.

From the twelfth century, the church was only partially concerned with religion. The clergy were involved in a range of activities, ranging from ambitious building projects, farming and law to medicine, welfare and education. A poem such as John Barbour's *The Bruce*, written within a generation of Bannockburn, stands out as being the sole representative of a poetic generation, earning Barbour the title of father of Scottish vernacular poetry. Politically, his romanticised valour is seen as offering an example to the leaders of his day, an example they did not follow.

During the high days of Roman Catholicism, God was hidden in the Latin language, making him inaccessible to ordinary people. Those who commanded the Word of God commanded the country. Both points fuelled the reformers' zeal; and the arrival of printing saw words multiply in their millions and burst upon the world.

When printing was invented in the fifteenth century the word became secular and the church could no longer remain the guardian of truth. Printing allowed the written word to be produced and copied with a speed that saw new ideas travel rapidly across Europe. So it's not surprising that the Catholic Church, by now weak and corrupt, felt threatened.

Most Scots poets had church connections and by the time we reach a remarkable poetic generation at the end of the fifteenth century, the associations are clear. Robert Henryson died in 1490; William Dunbar disappears after Flodden in 1513; Gavin Douglas died nine years later; and Sir David Lyndsay of the Mount died in 1555.

Some said he maid ane tomb of merbell gray,
And wrait hir name in superscriptioun,
And laid it on her grave quhair that scho lay,
In goldin letteris, conteining this ressoun:
'Lo, fair ladyis, Cresseid, of Troyis toun,
Sumtyme countit the flour of womanheid,
Under this stane, lait lipper, lyis deid.'
From *The Testament of Cresseid* by Robert Henryson

Henryson's *The Testament of Cresseid* is one of the masterpieces of Scottish literature. It is driven by a profound sense of pity for erring humanity, is emotionally blurred and morally inconclusive, urging women to heed Cresseid's life, and ending, 'Sen scho is deid, I speik of hir no moir.'

Henryson graduated from Glasgow University and was headmaster of the abbey school in Dunfermline. Little else is known about him; and not much more is known about William Dunbar, other than he may have been a Franciscan monk and was court poet to James IV. With Burns and MacDiarmid he is one of Scotland's greatest poets. Such is the force of his writing that after more than 600 years his personality comes through.

I will no priestis for me sing,
Dies illa, dies irae;
Nor yet na bellis for me ring,
Sicut semper solet fieri,
But a bag pipe to play a spring.
From *I maister Andro Kennedy* William Dunbar

His work is divided between secular and religious verse and though he can be both bawdy and dismal, thoughts of Heaven are never far away, especially when he considers how death has taken the poets he admired:

Our plesance heir is all vane glory,   presence
This fals warld is bot transitory,
The flesch is brukle the fend is sle: brittle; slender
Timor mortis conturbat me.
From *Lament for the Makaris* William Dunbar

His use of the tolling Latin refrain at the end of each verse is almost liturgical.

Douglas' translation of Virgil's *Aeneid*, the first in Britain, was done when he was Bishop of Dunkeld. But such works of devotion were created in a climate of mistrust. And by the time Sir David Lyndsay came along, comments were not so veiled. Four hundred years ago, a good Scottish household had Lyndsay's works alongside the Bible. And while one contained the Word of God, within the other was a blatant attack on the church.

Sir David Lyndsay belonged to a land-owning Fife family and was closely associated with the Scottish court, mainly due to his diplomatic work and travels in England and France. And though his political fortunes vacillated, his head and shoulders are carved into the fabric of Falkland Palace.

Throughout his work Lyndsay maintained the concept of divine benevolence, while criticising the church and state. In *The Dreme*, written in 1528, his depictions of Hell focus on the clergy, especially for their abuse of privilege and sexual misconduct. And later in *The Complaynt*, he targets the church, which has become so corrupt:

. . . thay may nocht thole the lycht   allow
Of Christis trew Gospell to be sene,
So blyndit is thare corporall ene   human eyes
With wardly lustis sensuall   worldly sensual lusts
Takyng in realms the governall,   governing
Baith gyding court and Cessioun,   session
Contrar to thare prefessioun,   against

Quarcof I think they sulde have schame
Off spirituall preistis to tak the name.
From *The Complaynt of*
Schir David Lindesay Sir David Lyndsay

In *The Testament of the Papyngo*, written in the early 1530s, Lyndsay offers sympathetic advice about courtly difficulties, and suggests he varies his approach from that of his predecessors. Papyngo's position as a parrot gives her a privileged position from which to comment, and in the final section she directs her anger against the clergy.

In *The Dreme*, John the Commonweill leaves, vowing to return when Scotland is well governed. He appears some twenty-five years later in Lyndsay's *Ane Pleasant Satyre of the Thrie Estaitis*, written in 1552, at the point in the play when his demands have been met.

Ane Pleasant Satyre of the Thrie Estaitis is the most important surviving drama of early Scottish literature. In the play, one of the characters, Spiritualitie, who is representative of the church, holds out against any kind of reform, illustrating Lyndsay's premise that the church is the most corrupt establishment of the realm. The play was performed in Cupar in 1552 though an amended version was played before the king and queen at Linlithgow Palace on Twelfth Night, 1540. Some of the comedy and sexually explicit references were omitted from the Linlithgow performance and again when the play was performed before the Queen-Regent, Mary of Guise, at Edinburgh.

Lyndsay urges reform. In its use of symbolism and choice of language it's both a violent and very funny play. The novelist, poet and short story writer, Alan Spence, who recently adapted the piece, says: 'The second act is largely a debate between John the Commonweill, in other words, the people of Scotland, who engages in a rant against the powers that be in the form of the Lords Temporal, and particularly the Lords Spiritual. At one point he screams at this Bishop who represents spirituality: "The fiend fart in your face!" It's as direct, as earthy and as rich as that. Lines like that still get a response from an audience.'

Satire was a risky business. Sixteenth-century critics of the church and state were regularly burned at the stake. Apart from intermittent wars with England, which caused widespread famine and discontent, the murder of Cardinal David Beaton on his way to St Andrews intensified the religious strife, especially since he left a mistress and several children. Lyndsay's genius wasn't just literary; it took a rare intelligence to raise a dissenting voice and survive.

Alan Spence agrees: 'Lyndsay's warning shot was meant to be heard. In effect, they didn't listen and the Reformation came along, and then things changed even more drastically than Lyndsay would have imagined.'

So the Catholic order collapsed and Calvinism formed the basis of the Presbyterian Church in Scotland. Rather than the church and its teachings being central to thought and action, Calvinists believed man could communicate with God directly and needed no intercession from the church or its hierarchy. There were three main tenets: 1) The majesty and power of God and the weakness and futility of man; 2) The authority of the Bible and the unquestionable nature of divine law; 3) Forgiveness of sins through love of Jesus Christ.

With the Bible as the authority, there was no need for the church to dictate to its congregation, and with Christ's forgiveness freely given there was no need for confession or third party intercession.

In the seventeenth century, Calvinism was modified to include the dogma of predestination, the belief that a man was either one of the 'elect' or a 'reprobate'; that is, he was either chosen by God for salvation, or doomed for eternity. There was no third way.

Scotland was divided into parishes. Every parish had a school and a church, with the minister often serving as the schoolmaster, or dominie. The level of literacy in Scotland increased dramatically, since Calvinism required its followers to read the Bible. Ironically, this was paralleled by a decrease in the range of writing available, since the kirk suppressed writing that did not conform to Calvinist ideology.

But where was God in all of this? Religious reformers such as John Knox felt that God had taken a back seat for too long. It was time for Him to take centre stage. Under the stern theocracy that followed the Reformation of 1560, Scotland's theatres were closed. Literature in Scotland almost died as a consequence. For Kenneth White the influence of Calvinism on art and literature was devastating: 'It killed minds and it restricted culture,' he said.

Of course, this is not how Calvinist reformers would have described their great project. Under John Knox's guidance, literacy and education were obviously encouraged. For the first time ever, ordinary people could study the Scriptures at home. In theory, Knox and his followers wanted people to think for themselves, but they had a deep mistrust of imagination. It was the way of the devil, a point A.L. Kennedy develops: 'Even if the writing isn't overtly political, being free inside your head is fundamentally subversive; so of course John Knox wouldn't like the creative act.'

James Robertson sees the devil looming large in people's lives: 'Not so much because he's associated with reading, because, after all, one of the driving forces of the Reformation was to give people access to the Bible in their own tongue, to give people a more direct access to God. In a sense the devil is hanging around there on the fringes because he is representative of an older kind of superstition. He's representative of the kind of thing that gets in the way of your relationship with God, and he's almost a figure that stands for the temptations that can divert you away from that relationship.'

And for Chris Dolan: 'The idea of no man between me and my God, the idea of it is you, and you alone, and you have a responsibility to yourself and to those round about you, and that you must make your peace with the Godhead, with the Cosmos, is extraordinarily revolutionary, and I think it sent Scotland on a literary, artistic and imaginative path which wouldn't otherwise have happened.'

Revolutionary Calvinism, which had set out to free the human spirit, quickly became a reactionary force that suppressed ideas at variance to their own. The kirk became an instrument of fundamentalism and sought to control society. Criticism of the God-ordained regime could still cost a life, so it's hardly surprising literature suffered.

Theatre was an immediate casualty. Besieged by the kirk's intolerance of the arts, the stage became a no-go area for almost 200 years. By putting false words into the mouths of men, playwrights were said to be mocking God's greatest creation.

The stage was seen as prejudicial to the interests of religion and morality; and just as the kirk's supporters had burned Roman Catholic churches, cathedrals, monasteries and abbeys, they now burned theatres. Actors were often arrested as vagrants.

Even as late as the eighteenth century, the kirk was grimly intolerant of imaginative literature. But no one was being burned for heresy, which might have encouraged Allan Ramsay to put his head above the theological parapet.

Allan Ramsay, master wigmaker with literary pretensions, was busted in 1725 when his bookshop and lending library, the first of its kind in the United Kingdom, was raided by Edinburgh magistrates. They objected to 'all the villainous, profane and obscene books and playes printed at London by Curle and others, are gote doune from London by Allan Ramsay, and lent out for an easy price, to young boyes, servant weemen of the better sort, and gentlemen, and vice and obscenity dreadfully propagated'. Ramsay had been warned.

Unperturbed, he pressed ahead with his own play, *The Gentle Shepherd*, a pastoral piece set in a village where neither laird nor kirk plays a significant part. He opened a theatre in Carrubbers Close and though the play appealed to a wide public, the kirk hated it and Ramsay was forced to close. Despite losing a fortune, he'd won a moral victory and within ten years Edinburgh had its own theatre, where the real scandal emerges in 1756 when a play is performed that had been written by a Church of Scotland minister, *The Tragedy of Douglas* by John Home.

The Tragedy of Douglas is both Home's personal challenge to religious hardliners and an attempt to put Scotland back on the artistic map. It provoked an outcry. *Douglas* was premiered at the Canongate theatre and although a text of the play survives, few can remember a line. The most memorable part of the evening came when a member of the audience was so enchanted he delivered the immortal line, 'Whaur's yer Wullie Shakespeare noo?'

Despite the play's success, the kirk came down on their own. Not only was Home forced to resign, but any minister who attended the performance was similarly censured. His friend and fellow minister, Alexander Carlyle, nicknamed Jupiter because of his noble bearing, apologised, then wrote an ironic satire, which he published anonymously: *An Argument to Prove that the Tragedy of Douglas ought to be Publicly Burnt by the Hands of the Hangman.*

The struggle against Calvinism continued. The kirk still believed in predestination: the idea that God has decided which souls to save, His elect, and the rest, comprising the vast majority of humanity, are doomed for all eternity. In this way Calvinism created its own social and spiritual élite, which provided a rich source of material for writers like James Hogg and Robert Burns.

The Auchterarder Creed of 1717 decreed that the elect need not forsake sin because God had chosen them. In effect, they could do what they liked. The elect wore black and reprobates were forced to wear hodden grey. This was the absurdity and hypocrisy Robert Burns had in his sights and eventually exposed in *Holy Willie's Prayer.*

This poem is generally regarded as one of the greatest satires in European literature. Although it was written before the publication of Burns' *Kilmarnock Edition* in 1786, it was omitted due to the topicality of the satire. Burns wrote the poem following a quarrel between his friend, the lawyer Gavin Hamilton, the Mauchline minister William 'Daddy' Auld and the Presbytery of Ayr. Holy Willie is based on a local church elder, William Fisher.

O thou that in the heavens does dwell!
Wha, as it pleases best thysel,
Sends ane to Heaven an ten to Hell,
    A' for thy glory!
And no for ony gude or ill
    They've done before thee.

From Holy Willie's Prayer Robert Burns

From the first verse there is no doubt about Burns' intentions. He opens with a statement of Calvinist preordained salvation and damnation; and Willie assumes he is one of the elect. Everything else he says is from this position, most especially exposing the insular, monstrous egotism which accompanies the doctrine. In the second verse Willie praises God approvingly. 'I am here,' he tells his creator; proof enough of God's goodness.

The most extraordinary testimony to Burns' genius is in choosing an interior monologue to reveal Willie's thinking thus giving his creation an opportunity to condemn himself. He allows us access to his thinking. Having insisted he is an example of God's chosen, he tells God 'vile self gets in' then admits sexual indiscretions, three times when drunk, which either sabotage his theory of divine certainty, or expose God's judgement as defective.

But yet, O Lord! confess I must –
At times I'm fash'd wi' fleshy lust;
An sometimes too, in warldly trust,
    Vile Self gets in;
But thou remembers we are dust,
    Defil'd wi' sin.

From Holy Willie's Prayer Robert Burns

Willie, of course, assumes God is interested in these indiscretions, obviously believing Mauchline is forever in the Almighty's thoughts, as a place in which the creator of the universe takes a special interest. Of course, God's to blame. He allows sexual temptation to come Willie's way because he is 'sae gifted'.

Burns maintains our interest by keeping Willie's smugness in his sight, finally coaxing him into doing something he's suggested from the start. By condemning the perpetrators of his outrage and calling on God to damn them eternally, Willie casts God in his own image. God is thus the creator of Calvinism, rather than anything else.

And Willie expects his rewards here on Earth as well as in Heaven. Being one of the chosen with an eternity of joy in prospect isn't enough. He wants it now.

Margaret Elphinstone agrees: 'In order to hold to the doctrine of the elect, and to assume that you are one of the elect you have got to be one huge hypocrite. And if you can't see that, then you can't even begin to relate to any other human being, or the world you're in.'

Andrew O'Hagan goes further: 'Scottish literature illustrates better than any literature I can think of the truth of the fact that you can do a thousand things more with humour than you can do with a censorious, serious blow. And that's certainly true about Burns and his attitude to religion. *Holy Willie's Prayer* is hilarious. It's a hilarious anti-doctrinaire, anti-fundamentalist poem that should be read to children to allow them to understand the scope for human freedom when faced with a blank, grey, unloving unorthodoxy.'

Willie assumes God is an extension of himself and that he is party to knowledge of God's will and his intentions. He is so deluded that it is possible, despite the fact that he's a preposterous figure, to feel sorry for the man, in his arrogance and joylessness.

But Burns' anger at organised religion should never be confused with an attack on God, for in fact Burns had a highly developed sense of spirituality, as Chris Dolan points out: 'He rebels against the whole idea of there being one autocratic power, but he believes in something beyond, something mythic which keeps him within some kind of spiritual world. That's another reason why he's so important to us, and why he's still modern. We still struggle with those things, and maybe even fundamentally somewhere believe in a kind of a spiritual life, if not a religious one.'

And, as we've seen, an even more powerful attack on the kirk came with James Hogg's *The Private Memoirs and Confessions of a Justified Sinner* in 1824. It's a complex work of diabolic possession, theological satire and local legend. Again, the sins committed by an elect and therefore justified person in their eyes cannot imperil their hope of salvation, even if that sin is murder. And the concept of a split personality was taken up by other novelists, most famously by Robert Louis Stevenson in *The Strange Case of Dr Jekyll and Mr Hyde*.

In 1843 the kirk blew itself apart in the Disruption. Many of its ministers and flock, increasingly concerned at the modernisation, broke away to form the Free Church of Scotland, the Wee Frees. The kirk that had been the great unifying institution since the Act of 1707 was gone, and the General Assembly of the Church of Scotland, which many thought had substituted for a parliament as a place where representatives of the whole community could meet and discuss great national issues, was considerably weakened, its authority blunted. No contemporary writers recorded the imme-diacy of its passing. Rather we have Disruption rhymes like this anonymous piece from around 1850:

> The Wee Kirk,
> The Free Kirk,
> The Kirk without the steeple;
> The Auld Kirk,
> The cauld Kirk,
> The Kirk without the People.

When James Thomson was born forty years after the death of Robert Burns, his mother Sarah was on her own spiritual quest. She was a follower of the preacher Edward Irving and believed Christ's second coming was imminent. She believed in a Holy City where there would be no darkness, where God is everywhere and flowing though the city is a river called the Water of Life. Thomson absorbed this teaching then turned the whole thing on its head. The City of Dreadful Night, like Alasdair Gray's Unthank, is never in sunlight; sleepless people wander the streets with 'dead Faith, dead Love, dead Hope'. God does not exist, and the river is called the River of Suicides.

> They leave all hope behind who enter there
> One certitude whilst sane they cannot leave
> One anodyne for torture and despair
> The certitude of Death, which no reprieve
> Can put off long and which divinely tender
> But waits the outstretched hand to promptly render
> That draught whose slumber nothing can bereave.
>
> From *City of Dreadful Night* James Thomson

Thomson was born into crippling poverty, orphaned at an early age and brought up in Irving's Royal Caledonian Asylum in Islington. As a young man he fell in love with a teenage girl who died of tuberculosis. In all this suffering how could there be a loving God?

Wandering the streets of an imaginary city, the narrator is forced to accept the death of faith. In a key passage he tells how he wanders into a great cathedral. A man is preaching to the doomed congregation:

> And now at last authentic word I bring,
> Witnessed by every dead and living thing;
> Good tidings of great joy for you, for all:
> There is no God; no Fiend with names divine
> Made us and tortures us; if we must pine,
> It is to satiate no Being's gall.
>
> From *City of Dreadful Night* James Thomson

Andrew O'Hagan sees Thomson's poem as a crucial intervention: 'It turned things around. It showed the kind of night-sweats, the difficulty, the horror, if you like, a kind of darkness about our religious beliefs.'

> Here Faith died, poisoned by Charnel air
> Here Love died, stabbed by its own worshipped pair
> Here Hope died, starved out in its utmost lair.
> Here Faith and Love and Hope are dead indeed,
> Can life still live? By what doth it proceed?
>
> From *City of Dreadful Night* James Thomson

Thomson's atheism is his response to a world where the squalor of the newly industrialised cities mocked any idea of a loving God. For the first time a Scottish writer wasn't simply attacking the hypocrisy and oppression of the church, society or its institutions. He was questioning the existence of God himself.

His view seemed vindicated as the world moved into a century dominated by science, revolution and cataclysmic wars. Thomson may have written God's obituary but many refused to give up on the idea of a meaningful existence and invested their faith elsewhere.

In the 1920s reaction against the First World War lead many to find faith in political ideologies. As we've seen, in *Sunset Song* Lewis Grassic Gibbon examines a society in a decline that can only be rectified by socialism, and Neil Gunn makes a similar point in *The Silver Darlings*. With Hitler, Franco and Mussolini dominating European politics, MacDiarmid wrote his *Hymns to Lenin*, and many other writers were drawn to the socialist ideal.

Sorley MacLean was born into a deeply traditional and God-fearing community on Raasay in 1911. The experience of urban poverty shattered any faith that he might have had in a loving redeemer.

There has been on the streets of Glasgow
And on the streets of Edinburgh
And on the streets of London
The rotten wrack on filth
Poverty, hunger, prostitution,
Fever consumption and every disease:
They all grew on its side
It went to seed with sores.

From *An Cuillin* Sorley MacLean

Sorley believed salvation was at hand. The Gaelic poet Kevin MacNeil explains: 'I think Sorley saw in Communism a sense of realistic humanity that chimed with what was happening in the world in those days that he couldn't see in the Bible.'

By the late 1930s MacLean's politics were given a new relevance with the approaching war in Europe. As he would later write, 'Looking back I could see the miseries of the Industrial Revolution and Clearances. Looking forward the hopelessness of Europe under the Nazis and Fascists. I was convinced the only hope for Europe was the Red Army of Russia.'

His response was *An Cuillin*, an epic poem, which draws on the Gaels' history of suffering and has as its spine the mountainous landscapes of his youth. The Cuillins of Skye rise above history and spread from the Western Highlands across the world.

Beyond the lochs of the blood of children of men
beyond the frailty of plain and the labour of the mountain,
beyond poverty, consumption, fever, agony,
beyond hardship, wrong, tyranny, distress,
beyond misery, despair, hatred, treachery,
beyond guilt and defilement, watchful, heroic, the
Cuillin is seen rising on the other side of sorrow.

From *An Cuillin* Sorley MacLean

Kevin MacNeil sees the poem as 'A great overview of European history, encompassing literature, sociology, so many ideals Sorley had, and these were largely political ideals. He wanted to encompass the great sweep of European history as seen from a Leftist perceptive.'

Hopes that Communism could subvert God were doomed when the Soviet Union destroyed the democratic hopes of Poland in 1944. Many Communist sympathisers in the West had to revise their opinions, and for Sorley mankind's great hope had been betrayed. The noble ideals of Communism seemed suddenly empty:

> There was a time I thought
> If the Red Army came
> across Europe
> the tryst would not be bitter;
> that it would not be with a bonfire
> as was seen in Prague,
> and that it would not be the heroic student
> that would go up in smoke
> but the brittle fire-wood of money
> – a splendid heather-burning –
> with the lying oil of rulers
> daubed on every tip.
>
> From *Palach* Sorley MacLean

With the decline of the Kirk's stranglehold on sexual mores loosened, realistic portrayals of sex really began to penetrate Scottish writing. When writers like Catherine Carswell and Nan Shepherd explored female sexuality in a way the church would previously have found abhorrent and tried to suppress, now all they could do was condemn and bluster from the sidelines.

And while Thomson suggested the only way forward for the human race was mass suicide, with the Soviet Union growing more repressive and the message being split between Chinese and Soviet brands of Communism, something like half a century after

Thomson, Alexander Trocchi embraced a kind of nihilism, using the far more contemporary methods of sex and drugs.

Trocchi, with fellow travellers Alan Ginsberg and William Burroughs, was a voice of the 1960s' beat generation. Edwin Morgan remembers him well: 'When I was a very young lecturer, just starting my career at Glasgow University, he was in his last year doing English, so I got to know him very well. A brilliant student. We all knew something wonderful would come of it. He didn't in the end get a good degree because he was doing other things. He was taking a lot of benzedrine, and he had started a pig farm of all things, just before his finals. He was an interesting and strange character, but we all thought there was something pretty remarkable here.'

Trocchi was motivated by a vehement hatred of bourgeoisie morality and spent most of his adult life embracing his personal destruction. By the time he died in 1984 he had been a heroin addict for thirty years, writing pornography and prostituting his wife to pay for his fixes. After moving to Paris, Trocchi published *Young Adam*. The novel's existential themes are again picked up in *Cain's Book*, written six years later in New York.

Trocchi explores the godless universe first described by Thomson. In the modern age there can be no room for conventional morality or higher truth; only raw experience has validity. He investigates the alienation of a stranger in a city. His permanent outsiders find no relief from their bleakness. Everywhere is despair, introversion and personal indifference. Even sex is pointless and casual.

I had never seen such ugly thighs, nor ever imagined it like that, exposed for me in match light, the flaccid buttocks like pale meat on the stone stairs, the baggy skirt raised as far as her navel and with spread knees making a cave of her crotch, the match flickering and this first sex shadowy and hanging colourless like a clot of spider web from the blunt butt of her mound.

From *Cain's Book* Alexander Trocchi

Kevin MacNeil found the novel's power lay in the fact that it was honestly written rather than being due to sensationalism that came from the way Trocchi lived. 'The fact that he wrote so honestly makes it no accident that many of the great American writers of the time admired his work. He was living the life, for better or worse.'

The loss of identity and a personal quest for meaning occupied other Scottish writers. Archie Hind's *The Dear Green Place* follows the ambitions of a would-be writer, Mat Craig, who works in a slaughterhouse with men who are well read and caring. As we watch their ideals disintegrate, we are forced to ask if Craig's are any better. Alan Sharp and Gordon Williams, Robin Jenkins and George Friel asked similar questions, like Hind lamenting the loss of community, questioning the sense of belonging and accepting that a creative personal ambition may be tempered by betrayal. Trocchi's ideas would later be pursued by the likes of Alan Warner and Irvine Welsh. The themes explored by these writers can still be seen as a reaction to the legacy of Calvinism, which Andrew O'Hagan sees as ultimately destructive.

'The great Calvinist effort to stamp out art would offer lessons to the Taliban,' he says. 'To make literary experience a kind of witchcraft, or something beyond the pale, something outside of the higher order of religious thinking has been a terrible legacy in Scotland.'

It's a subject we can't ignore because it's still here. Writers still find Calvinism around them:

It was a day peculiar to this piece of the planet,
when larks rose on long thin strings of singing
and the air shifted with the shimmer of actual angels.
Greenness entered the body. The grasses
shivered with presences, and sunlight
stayed like a halo on hair and heather and hills.
Walking into town, I saw, in a radiant raincoat,
the woman from the fish-shop. 'What a day it is!'
cried I, like a sunstruck madman.

And what did she have to say for it?
Her brow grew bleak, her ancestors raged in their graves
as she spoke with their ancient misery:
'We'll pay for it, we'll pay for it, we'll pay for it!'

From Scotland Alastair Reid

And for Margaret Elphinsone: 'Writing about transgression, that is transgression against a perceived righteousness, a very hypocritical righteousness, that I think is still alive and well.

'In Janice Galloway's novel *The Trick is to Keep Breathing*, a number of pressures are put on Joy Stone because she doesn't conform. She's been Michael's mistress, she's anorexic, she's all the wrong things. And in her case, it's not the Kirk, it's the mental hospital, it's the doctors, it's the other teachers at her school, and at one point it's the minister at the memorial service telling her she's the wrong kind of human being. I think you can still see the long shadow of institutions imbued by Calvinism that are crushing this young woman.'

At the beginning Joy embodies a kind of nihilism, insofar as she has almost nothing left. She has lost the things that gave her identity. Her lover has drowned and she has lost her personal status. She is cut off from her friends and family. She is barely existing, yet, somehow, the very process of survival through breathing means she is still alive at the end of the process.

And while writers no longer attack Calvinism directly, as Burns or Hogg did, they nevertheless show the individual in relation to institutions where the mentality and mindset survives, whether it's the Kirk, the state, the mental hospital or jail.

'I think *The Trick is to Keep Breathing* is important because at first sight it seems as though it might be quite nihilistic,' says Margaret Elphinstone. 'What is there for Joy? It's so ironic, her name, and her life seems such a negation; she negates her own body with anorexia, she won't eat, she harms herself, she almost feels like a negative entity as she goes through the breakdown. The trick is to keep breathing means keeping hold on existence, on any kind of subjectivity.'

'The ending is not an obvious triumph. It's pretty ambiguous, all these metaphors of swimming, whether she can swim, whether she can keep breathing because Michael drowned. What does she get a hold of that makes it worth surviving? If there's really nothing, what then? Who can I be? What can I get a hold of? At the end she is going to survive. But it's tenuous.'

Margaret Elphinstone believes Janice Galloway has put a particularly Scottish slant on nihilism in terms of place, 'which I would read as containing the Calvinism that is inherent in that place, in that community, which is very recognisably Ayrshire.'

But not all Scottish writers rejected God completely. Muriel Spark's work continually stresses the importance of spirituality. She often takes her readers into a world without faith, where one sees or experiences faith as a destructive force, to show the meaninglessness of such an existence. Without faith, her human beings are utterly banal, unable to see beyond the endless tedium of suburbia and petty affairs. Or they engage in pursuits which appear meaningless but which disguise a malicious intent.

When Dougal Douglas M.A. (Edin.) arrives in Peckham his shape and dark looks are obvious. The horns on his head are not. He joins a textile firm as part of an Arts in Industry programme, aimed at bringing vision to the workers. Dougal brings tears, absenteeism, fraud, blackmail and murder:

'During my first week,' Dougal told Mr Willis, 'I have been observing the morals of Peckham. It seemed to me that the moral element lay at the root of all industrial discontents which lead to absenteeism and the slackness at work which you described to me . . . There are four types of morality observable in Peckham,' he said. 'One, emotional. Two, functional. Three, puritanical. Four, Christian . . . Take the first category, emotional. Here, for example, it is considered immoral for a man to live with a wife who no longer appeals to him. Take the second, functional, in which the principal factor is class solidarity such as, in some periods and places, has also existed amongst the aristocracy, and of which the main manifestation these days is the trade union movement. Three, puritanical, of which there are several modern variants, monetary advancements being the most prevalent guage of the moral life in this category. Four, traditional, which accounts for about one per cent of the Peckham population, and which in its simplest form is Christian. All moral categories are of course intermingled. Sometimes all are to be found in the beliefs and behaviour of one individual.'

'Where does this get us?'

'I can't say,' Dougal said. 'It is only a preliminary analysis.'

From *The Ballad of Peckham Rye* Muriel Spark

Norman MacCaig found spiritual consolation in the natural world. A staunch atheist, his exultation comes from landscape and animals, and nature's ability to renew itself continually surprises him. The humility that usually accompanies religious worship is transferred to MacCaig's wonder at his own place in the face of the beauty of the natural world.

> And grass is grace. And charlock
> Is gold of its own bounty.
> The broken chair by the wall
> Is one with immortal landscapes.
>
> Something has been completed
> That everything is part of,
> Something that will go on
> Being completed forever.

From *July Evening* Norman MacCaig

Most contemporary writers have a spiritual dimension, clearly evidenced in the work of George Mackay Brown, but surfacing in unlikely places, such as Iain Crichton Smith's *Putting Out the Ashes* or Edwin Morgan's *Message Clear,* which at first sight is a textual maze, offering visual difficulties that reflect its spiritually hopeful message. The certainties of previous generations are questioned, but for many the very question carries comfort, if not actual consolation:

> The twilight is a cathedral: a hymn
> to summer thumps against the rafters
> of the sky. The voices of the congregation
> are cold and clear as holy water.
>
> From *The Siege* by Tracey Herd

Whatever forces shape our literary imagination today's writers are no longer in thrall to the God of authoritative religion; but if God is dead, ignoring us or simply forgotten, it's left to literature to search for meaning and our place in the universe. The poet Tracey Herd is not alone in thinking there's room for spirituality in the material world. She sees religion as a benevolent influence. 'I think you have to have something positive to hold on to,' she says. 'I tend to subscribe to the God-is-in-everything school rather than seeing Him as a patriarchal figure.

'I tend to see religion as a benevolent, small-scale feature in my life, but an important one nevertheless. It attracted me because it's something you can build up for yourself. I don't subscribe to any particular belief; I'm not even a regular churchgoer. I wouldn't say I was a religious person, its just something that's there in the background and I have to have it to believe in. I couldn't function in a world where I thought there was no God.'

Belief has proved such a violent catalyst that in some cases it's taken years for literature to deal with the subject. In a country torn by endemic sectarianism, we have no defining work dealing with the divisions. And we may be expecting too much to anticipate its arrival. Writing comes with an individual agenda; and in a multi-cultural society, God no longer carries the certainties of old. Alan Spence's Buddhism and Leila Aboulela's Islam have not simply influenced their work, but have been at its heart, just as Christianity enthused, inspired and stimulated Columba.

Alan Spence grew up in post-war Glasgow in a heavily Protestant environment. He couldn't help but be aware of the sectarian divide.

'There are wonderful aspects to it,' he says. 'There's a very pared down rationalism, a kind of no-nonsense approach to religion which I think has its place. But what it lacks, and I think what I was craving as a child, was something more obviously devotional and celebratory. I mean I thought the Catholic Church was wonderfully exotic when I was a kid, all these rituals and ceremonies that seemed denied to me in the background I had known. At a certain point there was an obvious divide, which is probably partly my generation moving from the orthodox religions.'

He came of age in the 1960s, 'when we were exploring anything and everything, looking for the big answers to the big questions, and we weren't finding those in what the churches had become.

'I think we all have to ask the big questions. It's part and parcel of being human, it's what drives us, what makes life worth living, what raises us above the mundane. There's an Indian school of philosophy which was founded on the repetition of the one mantra, *Netti, Netti*, which is translated as, "Not this", "Not this", meaning whatever answers anyone comes up with, no, it's not that, it's something else; it has to be something more. That sounds like a negative response, but ultimately it's positive, recognising there's something transcended, something above the mundane, something that can't be easily encapsulated in the language or concepts we're used to, and that ultimately is a spiritual search.'

Which leaves a series of imponderable questions. If God's off the agenda we have to find the answers for ourselves. But if spirituality is anything, it's a sense of wonder and an openness to the big questions, which leaves us to make our own way along the road to eternity.

first one solitary star
then one by one they pierce
the darkening sky
      From *ah!* Alan Spence

Lost Voices

Suitor: There is nothing a man might do, with you to inspire
him. You make me wish to be a hero.
Hester: Do you really think that the charm of inspiring is
what any reasonable creature would prefer to be doing? To
make someone else a hero rather than be a hero yourself?

From *Hester* Margaret Oliphant

Any list of Scottish writers will be male-dominated. We don't have
to look far to find alternatives; from Mary, Queen of Scots and the
early Gaelic poets, not to mention the ballad carriers and informants, to this century's long and impressive list of women
novelists, it's obvious Scotland has produced great women writers.
But they've somehow slipped into the margins.

Margaret Elphinstone feels the number of talented, prominent
women writers working in Scotland today means we can reassess
the past: 'Have there always been writers like this in Scotland? And,
if so, why are they not in print? Why have we not heard about
them all along?'

Our earliest written poetry casts a set of heroic male figures; the
contribution played by women is minimal. And while considerable
research has gone into resurrecting lost women writers, the earliest
known pieces belong to the sixteenth and seventeenth centuries.

Oh little did my mother think,
The day she cradled me,
What lands I was to travel through,
What death I was to dee.

From *Marie Hamilton* (Anon.)

Balladry can claim to offer an alternative tradition. 'Anon.,' says Liz Lochhead, 'was a great woman writer.'

Ballads have influenced our finest writers, from Robert Burns, Walter Scott and James Hogg to Hugh MacDiarmid, though he later denied it, and Lewis Grassic Gibbon.

'There are hundreds of them,' wrote Edwin Muir, 'and they contain the greatest poetry that Scotland has produced. We do not know now who made them, or how they were made, for it took generations to cast them into the shape in which we now know them. They bring us back again to the Scottish people and its part in the making of Scotland; for it was the people who created these magnificent poems. The greatest poetry of most countries has been written by the educated middle and upper classes; the greatest poetry of Scotland has come from the people.'

Muir's continual reference to the poetry of the ballads pre-supposes his never having heard them sung, or that he considered the tunes unimportant. And, until relatively recently, ballad study had a literary bias.

'We should never forget that the ballad is a sung genre,' writes Emily Lyle, introducing her collection of Scottish ballads, 'with a whole musical dimension that is not caught by the printed text.'

The expulsion of tunes restructured the songs' identity; by removing their origins, the source singer was obliterated. Ballads were heavily censored. Features considered impertinent to Victorian mores were purged, and the *Whistle-Binkie* publications can be seen as an attempt to replace them in the popular consciousness with subjects more agreeable to the pervading taste police, who were never diffident when it came to expressing their opinions and judgements.

> There liv'd a maid in Canongate –
> So say they who have seen her;
> For me, 'tis by report I know
> For I have seldom been there.

But so report goes on and says,
Her father was a baker;
And she was courted by a swain
Who was a candle-maker.
From *The Rose of the Canongate* John Donald Carrick

Balladry is a specifically female form. The finest examples were generally transmitted by women, who learned them from their mothers, grandmothers, nursemaids and servants. Burns was influenced by a close friend of his mother's who had 'the largest collection in the country of tales and songs'. Anna Brown, a minister's wife from Falkland who died in 1810, was an important source to early collectors; Scott's main informant for *The Minstrelsy of the Scottish Border* was James Hogg's mother, Margaret Laidlaw; Gavin Greig's main informant was Belle Robertson; and Hamish Henderson's principal source was Jeannie Robertson (no relation to Belle).

There are many other women whose roles are not so clear, women like Robert Louis Stevenson's nurse Alison Cunningham (Cummy), 'the angel of my infant life', who 'did so much to make that childhood happy'. Cummy read to him and comforted him through 'interminable nights', often scaring him with terrifying stories which he acted out in his 'land of counterpane' and which obviously informed his later fiction.

When Francis James Child was compiling his monumental work on *The English and Scottish Popular Ballads*, he urged collectors to record even the barest fragment: 'Something must still be left in the memory of men, or better, of *women*, who have been the chief preservers of ballad-poetry.'

This work doesn't include songwriters such as Lady Caroline Nairne, whose songs like 'The Rowan Tree', 'The Laird o' Cockpen', 'Charlie is My Darling' and 'Will Ye No Come Back Again?' are still popular. Nor were women simple informants. In folk song women rarely adopt a subservient or secondary role. They are usually the main protagonists and many songs are written from a woman's perspective:

> First whan we cam tae Edinburgh toon
> We were a comely sicht tae see;
> My luve was cled in the black velvet
> And I masel in crammasie.
>
> From *Waly, Waly* (Anon.)

The subject matter deals with the diversity and limitations of female experience as well as their preoccupations. Often their role is implicit rather than directly stated. And the women are rarely in need of male protection. After being abducted and forcibly married, Eppie Morrie is dragged to bed by her new husband. By morning, he's forced to admit defeat:

> He's taen the sark frae aff his back
> And kicked awa his shoon,
> He's thrawn awa the chaulmer key,
> And naked he lay doon, lay doon
> And naked he lay doon.
>
> 'Haud awa frae me, Willie,
> Haud awa' frae me,
> Before I lose my maidenheid
> I'll try my strength wi' thee, wi' thee.
> I'll try my strength wi' thee:'
>
> From *Eppie Morrie* (Anon.)

Walter Scott started where Burns left off, collecting folk songs. He published *The Minstrelsy of the Scottish Border* in 1802 and encouraged his daughters to learn the songs. The influence of balladry in Scott's work is obvious; the ballad subjects – outlaws, family feuds, battles and ill-fated love – are often repeated in his novels.

Before Scott, the novel was a form written predominantly for young women. It is perhaps with his eye on this market that Scott included a number of strong female characters, who could have stepped straight from the ballad tradition.

In *Heart of Midlothian*, his seventh novel published with the by-line *The Author of Waverley*, Scott turns from noble male heroes to Jeanie Deans, a cow-feeder's daughter. *Heart of Midlothian* tells the story of Jeanie's walk to London to plead for a reprieve for her condemned sister. On her journey she encounters corruption and hypocrisy in the church, the law and the royal court.

Jeanie Deans is based on Helen Walker, who refused to lie in court to save her sister who was accused of murdering a child. When her sister was subsequently condemned to death, Helen Walker walked to London to seek a pardon.

Scott sets the novel in 1730, shortly after the first Jacobite rebellion, and Jeanie symbolises Scotland and its regeneration. While the shift from noble male hero to peasant heroine is a radical departure, like her predecessors, Jeanie is a figure outside the establishment, pitted against overwhelming odds. Again, Scots are encouraged to identify with an underdog.

One of the bestselling Scottish novels of the nineteenth century wasn't written by Scott. *The Scottish Chiefs* by Miss Jane Porter was published in three volumes in 1810 and relates the story of Bruce and Wallace. Scott is said to have told George IV on his visit to Edinburgh that *The Scottish Chiefs* was the parent to his Waverley novels and a work of genius. James Hogg was an admirer and the novel acquired many other nineteenth-century followers.

Set in the dark and remotely romantic past, the success of *The Scottish Chiefs* may well be attributable to the reading public's taste for all things Scottish following the conquests of Ossian, and the novel carries an epigraph by the bard: 'There comes a voice that awakes my soul. It is the voice of years that are gone; they roll before me with their deeds.' This may account for Napoleon's admiration and could certainly have brought the book to his attention.

It is the first epic on the scale of Scott and like him draws on history for its setting, though it's as cavalier with the events and details surrounding the characters as *Braveheart*! Wallace and Bruce plan to save the nation. Wallace is pure and good throughout and despite being betrayed by the aristocracy, he secretly marries the traitor's daughter.

William Wallace retired to the glen of Ellerslie. Withdrawn from the world, he hoped to avoid the sight of oppressions he could not redress, and the endurance of injuries beyond his power to avenge . . . secluded in the bloom of manhood from the social haunts of men, he repressed the eager aspirations of his mind, and strove to acquire that resignation to inevitable evils which alone could reconcile him to forego the promises of his youth, and enable him to view with patience a humiliation of Scotland, which blighted her honour, menaced her existence, and consigned her sons to degradation or obscurity. The latter was the choice of Wallace. Too noble to bend his spirit to the usurper, too honest to affect submission, he resigned himself to the only way left of maintaining the independence of a true Scot; and giving up the world at once, all the ambitions of youth became extinguished in his breast, since nothing was preserved in his country to sanctify their fires. Scotland seemed proud of her chains. Not to share in such debasement, appeared all that was now in his power; and within the shades of Ellerslie he found a retreat and a home, whose sweets beguiling him of every care, made him sometimes forget the wrongs of his country.

From *The Scottish Chiefs* Jane Porter

If Ossian was Jane Porter's starting point, it may equally have inspired Susan Ferrier and Mary Brunton. Both shared her partiality for the brooding parable.

Susan Ferrier's first novel *Marriage* was published in 1818 and netted her a fortune. She was born and grew up in Edinburgh, the youngest of ten children. Her father was a lawyer and a friend of Scott. *Marriage* was published four years after *Waverley* and also aims to please a Scots and English readership.

The book belongs to a class of fiction which drew attention to society's changing values: should one marry for love, money or reputation? Susan Ferrier was very good at highlighting inconsistencies in behaviour, manners and attitudes, as well as exposing the hypocrisies she saw around her.

'This choice piece – it represents a Chinese cripple, squat on the ground, with its legs crossed. Your ladyship may observe the head and the chin advance forwards, as in the act of begging. The tea pours from the open mouth: and till your ladyship tries, you can have no idea of the elegant effect it produces.'

'That is really droll,' cried Lady Juliana, with a laugh of delight; 'and I must have the dear sick beggar, he is so deliciously hideous.'

From *Marriage* Susan Ferrier

Ferrier is alert to superficiality and greed. She is especially sharp on matters of money, prestige and property. *Marriage* also provides a unique insight into the way Scotland was perceived in Britain; and is particularly acute when dealing with the Highland gentry, blind to events outside their window. Ferrier lived for a time at Inveraray Castle and initially planned to write *Marriage* in collaboration with her friend Charlotte Clavering, whose grandfather was the fifth Duke of Argyll. At Inverary, Ferrier's biographer notes, she met, 'eccentric old Scottish Lairds, taking snuff and speaking in thick Scots dialect. She met the spoiled, bored ladies of fashion and the mindless young people with plenty of money and nothing to do.'

Her portraits were drawn from life. And the Scottish framework exposed class barriers which were clearly visible at the time, in direct contrast to Jane Austen who never plunges below the level of gentry and whose works are innocent of Scots, peasants and the Irish.

Ferrier appears to have little time for romantic nationalism; and this, in turn, may account for her neglect. Scottish novelists of the time have been overshadowed by Scott. His work engulfs everything; and though he and Susan Ferrier were great friends, and he admired her work, Scott produced the type of fiction which is now taken to represent Scottish literature as a whole. Susan Ferrier's subtler analysis of social manners does not quite fit this perception.

It must have been disheartening for Ferrier; when *Marriage* was published anonymously, as was the fashion, London critics assumed it was the work of Walter Scott. It made no mention of 'the author of Waverley', which they felt was a publisher's oversight. And when the novelist Matthew Lewis heard Susan Ferrier was writing a novel he commented, 'I have an aversion to all female scribblers. The needle, not the pen, is the instrument they use most dextrously.'

Ferrier survived into her seventies and wrote the last of her three novels twenty years before her death, having decided writing was not a suitable profession for a woman. Her grave in St Cuthbert's Churchyard at the West End of Princes Street simply records that she was her parents' daughter.

Mary Brunton was a contemporary of Susan Ferrier and Jane Austen. Her heroines are forceful and direct. The dainty drawing-room cannot confine Laura Montreville, the central character of Brunton's first novel *Self Control.*

Born Mary Balfour in Orkney in 1778, her husband, Alexander Brunton, was a Church of Scotland minister whose first parish was in Bolton, East Lothian. Towards the end of their time there, Gilbert Burns, brother of the 'Heaven-taught ploughman', came to the area to manage a farm owned by Mrs Anna Dunlop, who had been his brother's friend and correspondent. He is buried in Bolton kirkyard with his mother, sister and three daughters. Alexander Brunton left Bolton in 1803 to take up a calling in Edinburgh, firstly at Greyfriars, then at the Tron Kirk in the High Street.

Self Control was published anonymously in 1810. Two hundred and forty copies were sold within a week of publication and a second edition was printed within a month. It is dedicated to Joanna Baillie.

Laura Montreville is something of a subversive figure, and, compared to the men in the novel, is decisive and determined. When her mother dies, she and her father leave their village, which might be Bolton, and visit Edinburgh on their way to London. They travel by sea and after trying to make ends meet by selling her paintings to London dealers, Laura's father dies bankrupt, leaving her to fend for herself.

The first edition ran to 500 pages and had 34 chapters. The book begins as autobiography, but quickly develops an entertaining storyline, with an unusual international sweep and wide array of characters, who are rather emblematic, but nevertheless larger than life. From the first Laura is described as having 'an active mind, a strong sense of duty, and the habit of meeting and of overcoming adverse circumstances', something which will later stand her in good stead.

Self Control has an implied critique of the upper classes and certainly abhors the moral standards of the time. While in Edinburgh Laura learns a certain time must elapse between an invitation and a visit and she does not understand how a lady could manage to be engaged for four meals in two days. The rake Hargrave, whom Laura meets in London, fathers an illegitimate child to a serving girl, who later dies. De Courcy pays for the child's support. Hargrave later abducts Laura to Canada. She escapes in a canoe, returns to England and is reunited with de Courcy.

Mary Brunton felt her book lacked unity, that some of the incidents were poorly connected. The American jaunt, she thought, was the best part of the book, but was still little more than an appendage.

However, *Self Control* had other admirers. On 30 April 1811, Jane Austen was correcting the proofs of *Sense and Sensibility*. She wrote to her sister Cassandra saying she had tried, without success, to find a copy of *Self Control*: 'I am always half afraid of finding a clever novel too clever – and of finding my own story and my own people all forestalled,' she wrote.

Eighteen months later, in another letter to Cassandra, her tone is different: 'I am looking over *Self Control* again,' she says, 'and my opinion is confirmed of its being an excellently-meant, elegantly-written Work; without anything of Nature or Probability in it. I declare I do not know whether Laura's passage down the American River, is not the most natural, possible everyday thing she does.'

And a year later, in November or December, 1814, writing to her friend Anna Lefroy, Jane declared her intention of 'writing a close imitation of *Self Control*' as soon as possible. 'I will improve upon it,' she says. 'My Heroine shall not merely be wafted down an American river in a boat by herself, she shall cross the Atlantic in the same way, and never stop till she reaches Gravesend.'

And though Jane's tongue may be firmly in her cheek, there are similarities between the rector's daughter and the minister's wife. Characters in their novels remain the same and operate within close parameters; only the names and certain circumstances change. Both women wished to conform to accepted codes of behaviour, and encouraged their characters, through self-discipline and integrity, to do the same. Society's codes are governed and dictated by virtue and reason.

At this season of the year, however, when Laura reached Edinburgh, she had little cause for apprehension. The noble streets through which she passed had the appearance of being depopulated by pestilence. The houses were uninhabited, the window shutters closed, and the grass grew from services in the pavement . . . As they passed the magnificent shops, the windows gay with every variety of colour, constantly attracted Laura's inexperienced eye . . . The next thing which drew Laura's attention was a stay-maker's sign.

'Do the gentlemen wear corsets,' she asked to Montreville.
'What makes you inquire?'
'Because there is a man opposite who makes corsets. It cannot surely be for women.

From *Self Control* Mary Brunton

In a letter to Joanna Baillie, where Mary explains her dedication, she tells the author of *Plays on the Passions*, which she greatly admires, 'The regulation of the passions is the province, it is the triumph of religion.'

The year after *Self Control* was published, Alexander Brunton applied for the professorship of Hebrew and Oriental Studies at Edinburgh University. He was born in Edinburgh, educated there and had six years' experience of preaching in the city. With the appointment came a change of address and the Bruntons moved to the New Town. Settled now and with the success of *Self Control* behind her, Mary began work on a new novel.

Discipline was published in 1814. Mary was concerned, finding it 'very unfortunate in coming after *Waverley*, by far the most splendid exhibition of talent in the novel way that has appeared since the days of Fielding and Smollet. What a competitor for poor little me! The worst of it all is, that I have ventured unconsciously on *Waverley*'s own ground, by carrying my heroine to the Highlands!'

She need scarcely have worried. The similarities worked in her favour and she had another overnight success. Four days after publication, her husband was awarded a Doctor of Divinity degree.

Mary began work on a third novel, *Emmeline*, but in the spring of 1818, at the age of thirty-nine, found herself pregnant. Writing came to a standstill as Mary became increasingly convinced the pregnancy would be fatal. Meanwhile, the doctorate had increased her husband's workload: he found himself torn between the demands of university, the publication of his sermons and the attentions of a wife who was preparing for death, arranging for obituary notices to be sent in her own handwriting and arranging tokens of remembrance to be given to friends. A son was stillborn on 7 December 1818 and Mary Brunton died twelve days later.

Among the many gestures of appreciation was a 47-line obituary poem by Joanna Baillie.

Sections of the public believed Joanna Baillie's plays had been written by Walter Scott, whose work formed the basis of the National Drama, a form peculiar to Scotland, which concentrated on Scottish subjects.

In fact, Joanna Baillie was the only significant Scottish playwright of her time. Scott became her close friend and she visited him at Abbotsford. He considered her a major Scottish dramatist and poet, and in the third canto of *Marmion* describes her as 'the bold enchantress'. After her *Plays of the Passions* had been successfully shown in London, Liverpool and Dublin, he compared her to Shakespeare; and when her play *The Family Legend* was performed in Edinburgh in 1810, Scott wrote a prologue.

> The bride she is winsome and bonny,
> Her hair it is snooded sae sleek.   tied in a ribbon
> And faithfu' and kind is her Johnny
> Yet fast fa' the tears on her cheek,
> New pearlins are cause o' her sorrow,   lace trimmings
> New pearlins and plenishing too;   furnishings
> The bride that has a' to borrow
> Has e'en right mickle ado.   a lot to do
> Woo'd and married and a'!
> Woo'd and married and a'!
> Isna she very weel aff
> To be woo'd and married and a'?
>
> From *Woo'd and Married and A!* by Joanna Baillie

Woo'd and Married and A'! became very well known and was widely published, along with *Tam o' the Lin*, which was based on a children's rhyme rather than the ballad. Joanna Baillie reworked an older song of the same name by Alexander Ross. Though she was one of the most celebrated poets of the nineteenth century, she is now best remembered for a few songs that have entered the tradition.

The mother thinks her daughter should be grateful – 'The lassie is glaikit wi' pride.' She had nothing when she married and the girl should take to the spinning wheel and work hard since 'the gear that is gifted, it never/Will last like gear that is won.' Her father thinks, 'She's less o' a bride than a bairn.' Her husband to be, a lad 'frae the heather' is as callow as herself. The girl's in her teens and when her father thinks of her married, he's as likely to laugh as to cry. The bridegroom tells her he finds riches looking into her eyes and when he asks if she regrets her decision, the girl blushes, smiles and plays with her sleeve. Then, 'aff like a mawkin she flew'.

Ross' original took the mother's line and censured the bride for her lack of seriousness. By changing the emphasis, Joanna Baillie says as much as her contemporaries did on marriage.

She had had a sheltered childhood as the daughter of a Lanarkshire minister. Her mother was Dorothea Hunter Baillie, sister of the Hunter brothers, the pre-eminent physicians of the day.

John Hunter is recognised as the father of comparative anatomy. As an army surgeon he gathered a collection of more than 13,000 human and animal specimens, which became the basis for the Royal College of Surgeons' collection, where his work and pioneering studies can still be seen.

His elder brother William created the Hunterian Museum and Art Gallery at Glasgow University, where he'd studied divinity, before moving to Edinburgh to study medicine. He founded his own school of anatomy, was appointed physician to Queen Charlotte and published the first gynaecological textbook. He also published the first English language pathology textbook and is buried in Westminster Abbey.

A career in medicine was inconceivable for Joanna Baillie or her sister Anna, who became Joanna's lifelong companion. Her father, who was Professor of Divinity at Glasgow University, died in 1778, and when Matthew went to Oxford, the sisters and their mother stayed on the Hunter family estate at Long Calderwood, near East Kilbride, eventually moving to London in 1783. Shortly after Joanna's first collection of poetry was published, the sisters moved to Hampstead, where they stayed for the rest of their lives.

Joanna Baillie's first volume of plays was called *A Series of Plays; in which it is attempted to delineate the stronger passions of the mind.* Her *Plays of the Passions* had a reputation for being tempestuous and fiery. When Byron was dining with his banker in St James's Place, he compared Scott and Baillie in the same breath. Voltaire reckoned, 'The composition of a tolerable tragedy requires testicles.' Byron used this comment in a letter in 1817 adding, 'Goodness knows what Joanna Baillie does – I suppose she borrows them.'

Byron tried to sponsor Baillie's work in London, especially with the theatre in Drury Lane, just as Scott sponsored her in Edinburgh. The Reformation had all but stamped out theatre in Scotland. Two centuries later when Baillie began to write it was still regarded with suspicion, so it took a courageous, determined woman to become a playwright. Liz Lochhead admires Joanna Baillie enormously: 'For her to pick up the writing of plays is a strange and a rather wonderful aberration.'

Baillie's twenty-eight plays were performed regularly over the first three decades of the nineteenth century. *De Montfort* opened in London's Drury Lane in 1800, toured in Scotland and was played as far afield as New York.

It wears, methinks, upon the midnight hour.
It is a dark and fearful night; the moon
Is wrapped in sable clouds: the chill blast sounds
Like dismal lamentations.

Are there not wicked fiends and damned sprites,
Whom yawning charnels, and unfathomed depths

Of secret darkness, at this fearful hour,
Do upwards send, to watch, unseen, around
The murderer's death bed, at his fatal term,
Ready to hail with dire and horrid welcome,
Their future mate? – I do believe there are.

From *De Montfort* Joanna Baillie

Her work was performed by the great actors of the day, Robert Kemble and Sarah Siddons. But despite her popular success she felt harshly judged by the critics.

The National Library of Scotland has a number of her letters. In a volume of correspondence to Scott, I came across a letter written from Hampstead on 13 October 1826. She describes herself as despondent and gloomy. 'I tire of reading,' she says, 'for I never was by nature a reader and have no heart to write.' She feels she has to take herself 'to a spinning wheel for the sake of the motion and the noise, or go out to tea parties, or coax my neighbours to come in to me and play at backgammon, poor expedience all of them.' She apologises for her gloomy tone and ends by saying she must 'speak feelingly on this subject, like a burnt child. John Anybody,' she says, and she underlines the word Anybody, 'John Anybody would have stood higher with the critics than Joanna Baillie.'

Despite the fact that she was acknowledged in her lifetime as *the* female writer of the age, Joanna Baillie's work has been forgotten and, regrettably, it is unlikely to stumble back into favour. She deserves to stand higher than John Anybody. Her works present an alternative Scotland to that promoted by Scott and his imitators. Many of her plays are set in shadowy castles occupied by dashing, noble savages who have more than a passing resemblance to Ossian, and her language is far from conventional. As can be seen from *Woo'd and Merrit an' A!*, she understands the oral tradition perfectly.

Her plays seem to typify the taste of the time. Elements of her plots are far-fetched, there appears to be pages of pointless versification, interspersed with sudden and dramatic bursts of action. They are very ambitious and their stage effects can be exciting, full of a surprising passion, with thunder and lightning storms. Characters are sharply drawn. Passions that can control and dominate one's life must be kept in check. There are discussions on the purpose of these passions and the morality needed to keep them at bay. If they are not mastered, downfall, chaos and disorder result.

The nineteenth century brought a degree of emancipation and financial freedom to upper- and middle-class Scotswomen and these changes in society are clearly reflected in Margaret Oliphant's work.

Born Margaret Wilson at Wallyford, near Edinburgh, in 1828, she published her first novel at twenty-one. Four years later her fourth novel, *Katie Stewart*, was serialised in *Blackwood's Magazine*. This was the start of a business relationship which ended with her death in 1897.

The year before she established the Blackwood's connection, she moved to London and married her cousin, the artist Francis Oliphant. He died in 1857, leaving her with three children and heavily in debt. From then she produced an average of two novels a year, including a seven-volume series called *The Chronicles of Carlingford*, closely modelled on Trollope's Barsetshire books.

Oliphant's fiction is notable because of her central female characters' autonomous spirit. Her portrayal of Kirsteen as an unselfconsciously independent woman led to her books being called novels without heroes.

It was strange to be in the thronged and noisy streets full of people, more people than Kirsteen had supposed to be in the world, going through the strange town to see Anne, that was the climax of all strangeness. Anne whose name was never named at home whom everybody remembered all the more intensely because it was forbidden to refer to her. Anne who had gone away from her father's house in the night leaving the candle flaring out in the socket and the chill wind blowing in through the open door. Something of the flicker of the dying candle was in the blowing about of the lights along the long range of the Trongate, above that babble of noises and ever shifting phantasmagoria.

From *Kirsteen* Margaret Oliphant

Kirsteen is remarkable. She is a Victorian woman without a man waiting in the wings. Her sisters think any man is better than none. Kirsteen believes in true love and is prepared to wait. She has an idealistic view of love and honour. When her fiancée dies in India with Kirsteen's handkerchief pressed to his lips, she is left to get on with her life.

Kirsteen believes in the family and in helping those members less fortunate than herself. But for Oliphant, women's changing social conditions came at a price. It was perfectly acceptable that she should run her own household when her husband died, but she was forced into hack journalism to support her two sons, who sponged off her all their lives. She reviewed all the great novelists, preferred Thackeray to Dickens, admired George Eliot and the Brontë Sisters, with some reservations, and approved of Stevenson and Barrie. She also helped her two brothers – one an alcoholic, the other with mental health problems – and continued to support their families when they came to grief, leaving very little time for herself or her work.

'She says somewhere that she actually wore a hole in her finger by writing, writing, writing all the time,' says novelist Moira Burgess. 'She thought herself, and it is thought now, that she could have written more and better novels if she hadn't had to keep the hack work going. The way she had to live really weighed her down, caused her even to doubt her own abilities, which I think is about as sad a thing as can happen to a writer.'

Virginia Woolf was led 'to deplore the fact that Mrs Oliphant sold her brain, her very admirable brain, prostituted her culture and enslaved her intellectual liberty in order that she might earn her living and educate her children.' Barrie, Thomas Carlyle and

Henry James, on the other hand, admired the potential they found in her work.

Edwin Muir described his meeting with Willa Anderson as 'the most fortunate event in my life'. It happened in September 1918 when she was visiting Glasgow and he was working as a shipping clerk. They married within the year, and, spurred by his wife's encouragement, the couple moved to London where Muir began writing full-time. She was particularly supportive of Edwin's poetry, especially during his worsening psychological state. Muir felt oppressed by London and underwent analysis, which became central to his poetry and shaped his view of the world.

In 1921 the Muirs moved to Europe, firstly living in Prague, then in Germany, Italy and Austria. They collaborated in translating modern European authors, notably Franz Kafka, bringing all his work into English and introducing him to a world audience. Their Penguin translations are still in print. In all they translated more than forty books, mostly from German. Willa was the better linguist and did most of the work.

While in Europe they began writing novels, and Willa's first novel *Imagined Corners* was published in 1931. It established what were to become lifelong themes: childhood, a sense of belonging and the suffocating nature of small town life, based on her childhood in Montrose, a time she later called 'a soft strangling'.

Mabel was feeling restless. Calderwick was a dull little hole, she reflected . . . It was colourless – grey skies, grey pavements, grey people. She herself would become grey in the course of time. Sarah Murray, she thought with a flash of spitefulness and horror, was grey already, inside if not out, although she was only a little over thirty. Mabel looked down at the silken sleeve of her rose-coloured gown. Then she walked deliberately up to her bedroom, turned on the lights and drew the curtains.

From *Imagined Corners* Willa Muir

Willa maintained her novels were written for money and when it didn't materialise, she turned to other sources of income, notably translation. She regretted nothing. After Edwin died in 1959, she wrote *Living with Ballads*, which he'd been commissioned to write, and a short memoir, *Belonging*, which concludes: 'That was the end of our Story. It was not the end of the Fable, which never stops, so it was not the end of Edwin's poetry, or of my belief in true love.'

Each of the characters in *Imagined Corners* needs freedom to find themselves, to establish their personal beliefs and follow their instincts. She urges her characters to take risks and to live by their discoveries. Also implicit is the ways in which men and women stand apart, the ways they limit their experience and guard themselves from one another.

In Willa Muir's second novel, *Mrs Ritchie*, Anna Ritchie identifies her sexual self with Satan, seeing body hair as a mark of the Devil, imposed at puberty. She does not respond to her husband sexually and eventually stops speaking to him. She beats her infant son when he has an erection and banishes him from the house when she is breastfeeding his younger sister. She believes she has been chosen, that her trials have brought her closer to God, making her one of his elect. She has never willingly given way to passion. Her place in Heaven is therefore assured. She has become split, like Hogg's Justified Sinner, dividing herself from love and life; and, for the first time, the Devil is presented as a woman.

It would be interesting to speculate to what extent Willa was influenced by her friend Catherine Carswell, one of the most controversial women novelists of the early twentieth century.

Her first novel, *Open the Door*, was published in 1920. Joanna Bannerman is a capricious and warm-hearted girl who comes to study at Glasgow School of Art. She finds the city promises more than her evangelical background considered possible, far less proper. Joanna reaches for what she calls loveliness and discovers an emotional and sexual awakening.

The young man's lean wrists and his long fingers, so dark and merciless, thrilled the child to the soul. Secretly she imagined herself a fluttering little bird in their cruel yet skilful grasp; and she felt she would gladly have let them crush the life out of her for their own inscrutable ends.

Actually one wet afternoon it looked as if her fantastic wish might come true. She and Gerald were in the coach-house . . . and for perhaps half an hour she had been watching in rapt silence while a pearly-breasted chaffinch was stuffed and sewed up. But, suddenly tired of his finicking task, Gerald threw down his work and stretched his arms above his head with a groan. He was sitting on the worn bench by the door, with his back to the dripping eaves, and presently to amuse himself he drew Joanna between his knees. Smiling, he pointed his penknife that was still blood-stained against the child's breast, almost cutting through the wool of her faded, tightly stretched jersey, and he threatened to skin her like a little bird. To his surprise – for he expected her to wriggle or protest – Joanna stood dumb and quite still and strange in his grip. So he soon stopped teasing her. But he had provided her with a theme which she afterwards embroidered out of all recognition in many an erotic rhapsody.

From *Open the Door* Catherine Carswell

Margaret Elphinstone thinks the way she represents Joanna's sexuality 'really puts on the line that sort of female subjectivity, and says things that have not been said. I think it's a very important book.'

Carswell was born in Glasgow in 1879 to a prosperous, God-fearing, middle-class family. Her son John tells us that the opening chapters of *Open the Door* mirror exactly his mother's life. She attended literature classes at Glasgow University, at a time when women couldn't graduate, and later studied music at Frankfurt Conservatory. Her first marriage in 1904 ended after her husband tried to kill her and he was subsequently declared insane. Carswell won a groundbreaking test case to have the marriage annulled.

Her second marriage to the journalist Donald Carswell was a success. One of their joint projects was a delightful collection of poems, extracts, songs, recipes and quotations, *The Scots Weekend*, designed by them for holiday pleasure. It shows an enviable breadth of reading and a genuine love for the subjects and country as a whole. 'Our wonder,' they say, 'is that we have so much to show.'

Catherine Carswell lost her job as a book reviewer with the *Glasgow Herald* in 1915 because of D.H. Lawrence's novel *The Rainbow*. Though she and Lawrence were friends, the review isn't exactly without criticism. 'It's difficult to define even to one's self what Mr Lawrence's aim actually is,' she says at one point. Lawrence's work was controversial, she feared the review might not be published and sent it straight to print, an act that would be severely censured today.

The novelist Alison Fell identifies with Catherine Carswell's independent character: 'She was always going to put her finger on painful and difficult, contiguous spots about Scottishness, repression, sexuality, womanhood. She would never be able to be accepted. She would always be slightly maverick.'

She wasn't alone. Nancy Brysson Morrison's approach is less direct and ultimately less hopeful because the weight of social convention and expectation is heavier. She came from a family known as 'the writing Morrisons'. Her brother Thomas and her sister Margaret were both novelists, Margaret writing as March Cost.

Nancy Brysson Morrison's first novel *Breakers* is set in a Highland manse where three sisters are trapped by circumstance, convention and geography. Their father is both dominant and feeble, and marriage presents their only hope of escape. She also presents an early fictional account of the Highland Clearances.

Morrison's third novel, *The Gowk Storm*, takes its title from a snow fall, 'a storm of several days at the end of April or the beginning of May'. The snowfall presages an early death and the novel follows the lives of three sisters over the period of a year. The lives of Julia, Emmy and Lisbet Lockhart are connected through conflict and desire. Duty compels Julia into a loveless marriage when her father forbids her to marry a Catholic. Emmy falls for a friend's fiancé and Lisbet narrates their story.

Their surname suggests restriction and frustration, and their stories unfold with an inevitability and economy. The girls are governed by a pattern of behaviour and religious certainty which ultimately destroys their lives. Their only escape lies in defiance, which is thwarted at every turn and runs counter to the Calvinist theory of pre-destination. By thinking for themselves, they run the risk of damnation by opposing God's will.

Like Carswell and Muir, Morrison writes beautifully. She imbues her characters' surroundings with a symbolism and imagery that is impressionistic and wonderfully effective, revealing a reality that is tragic in its familiarity.

Scottish women writers now seemed to offer hope rather than identification. Change became a persistent theme and ambition replaced confinement. The certainties and duties of the previous century were openly questioned. Women were encouraged to develop in ways a previous generation would have found unthinkable. The claustrophobia, narrow experience and restrictive social contact were challenged and condemned. Morrison's ending is dark and sadly inevitable; hope lies in Lisbet's departure.

As well as widening their range of social and political possibilities, women also had to alter the ways they were seen and especially the way they saw themselves. This was where the Scottish talent for inferiority blossomed. Scottish women writers have suffered from what has been called the double knot on the pinny. The first knot is the one all Scottish writers face in being perceived as part of a minority culture within Britain. The double knot comes when women writers are seen as second best within that context.

The woman who is to my mind our finest novelist, Muriel Spark, has never been granted the status she deserves. Nor has Liz

Lochhead's imagination, energy and range been fully acknowledged. Both writers have relentlessly altered our perceptions yet to a large degree have been taken for granted.

Jackie Kay is not alone in recognising Liz Lochhead's enormous influence: 'For somebody of my age, it was really nice to have somebody who had done that and been there. And you follow people like that. But for Liz Lochhead herself, who did she have? And it's that recent.'

For Liz, at times, it seemed as if she was inventing the wheel. 'Of course, that wasn't true,' she says. 'There had been various women writers, but they kept getting marginalised. I think I was very lucky because there was an actual hunger for a female Scottish voice when I started writing. Now, of course, there are loads of Scottish women writers, there are as many as men and so there should be, but even as recently as the early 1970s that wasn't true.'

Liz Lochhead is one of our most important writers, whose work has attracted a large and admiring public. Her poetry and drama are equally popular. Her readings are events. She has worked in revue and professional theatre and has directed her adaptation of Moliere's *Tartuffe*.

From her first poetry collection *Memo for Spring*, her work has been typified by vivid phrases where she explores meaning; how simple words and phrases can be misunderstood. She is also a keen observer of human behaviour, is especially good at detailing relationships from a woman's point of view and has a wonderful eye for detail.

She is especially fond of finding new meanings in ballads and folk tales, giving them a contemporary relevance:

National bird: the corbie, le corbeau, moi!
How me? Eh? Eh? Eh? Voice like a choked laugh. Ragbag o'a burd in ma black duds, a' angles and elbows and broken oxter feathers, black beady een in ma executioner's hood. No braw. But Ah think Ah ha'e a sort of black glamour.

From *Mary Queen of Scots Got
Her Head Chopped Off* Liz Lochhead

The range and variety of contemporary Scottish women's writing is extraordinary, reflecting the confidence found in Scottish writing itself. Kathleen Jamie turns centuries of Scottish thinking on its head by having the Queen of Sheba come to call, leading camels across football pitches and round the kirkyard, showing us how to eat exotic fruit:

> Sure enough: from the back of the crowd
> Someone growls:
> > Whae do you think y'ur?
> and a thousand laughing girls and she
> draw our hot breath
> and shout:
> THE QUEEN OF SHEBA!
> > From *The Queen of Sheba* Kathleen Jamie

Emotional distances, the ways social contact can be threatening and welcome are among a previous generation's themes that still concern Ali Smith. Her characters appear in transition, on the cusp of discovery, as if there is something they need to resolve, a past pain or future development. They are capable of dropping that which does not suit their mood or present identity and can leave at will, even on impulse.

Her stories seem closely personal, and, as with many gay writers, their sexuality can be ambivalent. The female protagonist could equally be male, especially in the way gender roles are investigated.

By having a transvestite take centre stage; by making Joss Moody begin as a girl who dresses as a man and is eventually accepted as a man, Jackie Kay erodes distinctions, suggesting progress may lie in ignoring gender differences to a point where they become extinct. Joss remains as she was throughout. Her transition is outward and centered on society's perception. He remains perfectly normal.

And while it would be pleasant to believe good writing stays alive and can live forever, the reverse is often true and some fine writers are unjustly forgotten. A.L. Kennedy reckons, 'There's still an idea that the Scottish marketable product will be grim and gritty and male. And you'll be reviewed under those terms; so it's still a little narrower for women to get in. A lot of voices are still missing. We're not fully representing the diversity of our culture. There are voices that aren't there and partly that's because a decision's been taken that these voices can't be sold.'

The Words We Use

As far as [literature] imitates at all, it imitates not life but
speech, not the facts of human destiny, but the emphasis and
the suppressions with which the human actor tells of them.
From *A Humble Remonstrance, Memories
and Portraits* Robert Louis Stevenson

Irvine Welsh's *Trainspotting* exploded into bookshops in 1993
and, with a cast of junkies, thugs and chancers, penetrated what
had previously been seen as a non-literary market. People whom
publishers, their publicists and booksellers thought were beyond
their reach bought *Trainspotting*.

And the film, which came along two years later, helped. Like the
book, it was located in a place hardly anyone recognised as
Edinburgh. This was Muirhouse, another Edinburgh, a schemey
Edinburgh far removed from Morningside and a setting rarely
portrayed in Scottish writing.

The seamy expedition wasn't all that was fresh. The originality lay in the way Welsh used language. He gave the
people a voice others recognised; and his muscular use of a
contemporary vernacular flew in the face of generations of
schoolteachers who belted children for not speaking properly,
and rejected the notion that language could be divided into
what was good and what was bad. It shocked those who
expected their writers to sound as if they'd been well brought
up.

Like most Scottish writers, Welsh began elsewhere: 'I started
writing in standard English and it didn't make sense to me. I just
wasn't hearing the voices in that way.'

He is one of a number of Scottish writers who by using their own voice follow a precedent set 300 years previously in the city Welsh reinvented.

Language isn't static; it's a living, growing, changing thing. As a dramatist, Liz Lochhead has to find the voice of each character: 'And many of these characters have used things I would probably call Scots, though some people might call it Kailyard keech or slang, but language has never been a pure thing.'

A point that raises what is for many the most contentious issue is addressed directly by Welsh: 'Somebody said, "There's too many fucks and too many cunts in the book." I says, "Well, how many is enough and how much is too many?"'

For a writer like Matthew Fitt, it isn't a matter of choice: 'I was brought up speaking Scots. I was also brought up getting Scots belted out of me. But it was the language I wanted to explore as a writer.'

'People like me, we were educated not to sound Scottish,' says A.L. Kennedy, who, like Matthew Fitt, was raised in Dundee. 'So you have slightly Scottish grammar and you have slightly Scottish concerns, but the language is standard English.'

Scottish writers are lucky. We have three languages to draw on. Scotland reinvented itself in the eighteenth century. The 1707 Act of the Union had a huge effect on our language and culture. The Union of the Crowns in 1603 and the departure of the Scottish court marked the beginning of the end of Scots as a national language fit for all spheres of activity; and the Union of the Parliaments accelerated the process.

Then came the era of the Scottish Enlightenment, of David Hume and Adam Smith, of invention, intellectual enquiry, debate and a flourishing culture. It was also a time of linguistic schizophrenia. English had become the standard for refined speech and was seen as dialectally emblematic of progress. Scots was associated with coarseness, a lack of gentility, barbarism; and Gaelic wasn't considered at all.

By 1761, the attitude was so prevalent that a group of Edinburgh intellectuals, known as the Select Society, felt it necessary to warn

Scottish gentlemen of the disadvantages to be suffered from their imperfect use of the English tongue. They proposed importing elocution teachers to tackle the problem.

And, as Alastair Reid points out, even Scotland's most eminent intellectuals fell within the tides of fashion. 'David Hume used to send his manuscripts to an English friend in Norwich to de-Scottify his prose. It was generally assumed that if you wanted to get on you'd better speak "the English".'

Janet Paisley finds the process far more sinister: 'The one thing that is unusual is that Scotland chose to give up its main language of business and education, and it did that around the time of the Union. After you've given up political power, what's to giving up your language? You might as well give up the whole idea that you're a Scot, which is effectively what the people did. They gave up the right to self-determination, and they gave up their voices.'

The Enlightenment and its by-products carried Edinburgh's name across Europe, which brought coachloads of visitors. On the evening of 4 November 1774 a young English gentleman, Henry Topham of York, arrived at the end of his Grand Tour to finish his education. At that time there were two dukes, sixteen earls, two countesses, seven lords, seven lords of session, five famous professors and two of the country's smartest boarding schools for young ladies all in the Canongate.

Topham loved Edinburgh, despite the climate, became pro-Scottish, and, after a shaky start, enjoyed the hospitality, believing there was little difference between here and France. There was, however, one thing he didn't like: 'Their pronunciation and accent is far from being agreeable; it gives an air of gravity, sedateness, and importance to their words; which though of use sometimes in a harangue or public discourse, in common conversation seems dull, heavy, stupid and inharmonious.'

Upwardly mobile Scots agreed. Topham approved of our use of the diminutive ending, but 'scarcely ever heard a Scotchman tell a good story'.

Those who wished to improve themselves by speaking 'like the

English' were, Topham said, 'the politer sort of people and the Professors of the College who, in their lectures, strive to shake off the Scotch pronunciation as much as possible'. Though, in the main, Scots wrote 'English like a foreign tongue, their mode of talking, phrase and expression but little resembling their works'.

Help was at hand. In 1779 the philosopher and anti-slavery campaigner James Beattie published a book called *Scoticisms* which he said was designed to correct the improprieties of speech, specifically for those souls who had no opportunity to learn good English from the company they kept. It became a bestseller and spawned a host of imitations.

Twenty years later, Hugh Mitchell, 'Master of the English and French Academy, Glasgow' published, at his own expense *Scotticisms, Vulgar Anglicisms and Grammatical Improprieties Corrected, With Reasons for the Correction.*

It's great. The Preface tells us that no matter how educated, there are those who 'have the mortification to find themselves better qualified for the caverns of a wilderness than for the society of men'.

They may be educated, but 'have still to learn that which is most essential, and which, in reality, is the only solid foundation of every other branch of Literature . . . That, to an Englishman, the English language is of more value than all the other languages in the world, dead or living, taken together. The reason is obvious. This alone is the language in which an Englishman thinks, and arranges his thoughts, and speaks, and transacts the affairs of life.'

Mistakes are listed alphabetically. We should never ask for a drink of beer. Drink means liquor of any kind, wine, rum, gin and so on; whereas draught means the act of drinking or the quantity of liquor drunk, therefore one should ask for 'a draught of beer'.

'He is flitted to George Square', should be, 'He has moved or has removed to George Square: To flit seems properly applicable to the migration of birds.'

'*Mask* the tea is Scotch; *infuse* the tea is English.'

'No colloquial idiom in Scotland is more common than *will I?*

instead of *shall I?* . . . If I say to a person, "Will I see you tomorrow?" His answer should be "It is impossible for me to be sure whether you *will* or *will not* see me tomorrow; for that you alone can know." An Englishman asks his neighbour, "Will *you* see me tomorrow?" or "Shall *I* see you tomorrow?" but the most illiterate Englishman never says, "*Will* I see you tomorrow?" '

Let's not forget, nobody did this to us; this is what we did to ourselves. This is a Scot telling other Scots how to be English.

Edinburgh itself was never more divided. The Old Town was a teeming mass of wynds, closes, taverns and whorehouses, a city virtually without streets. In contrast, the construction of the New Town, with its neo-classical buildings, geometric street plan and Anglicised street names symbolised order, progress and pride in the Union.

And from the Old Town closes came one of the most extraordinary writers of the day. Robert Fergusson died in Edinburgh six weeks before Henry Topham arrived, in a straw-littered cell, not yet twenty-four, having spent his last weeks raving and depressed, tormented by religious mania and locked in the Edinburgh madhouse at Bristo, next door to the poorhouse. He wrote searingly vivid and adventurous poetry, which reflected the Edinburgh he knew.

Edinburgh's poet laureate, Stewart Conn, is excited by the quality of Fergusson's writing: 'Having initially written in a rather effete if precise English, he switched and in his last three years produced living speech rhythms of the time. And the people Fergusson observed were not the politically correct people. They were the downtrodden; they were those in squalor. He described with incredible energy and with great formal finesse the sounds and the sights and smells of Edinburgh.'

Auld Reekie is the most vivid, authoritative picture of old Edinburgh, depicting a weekend, Saturday and Sunday in the city. Fergusson paints crowded drinking houses where friends take oysters, protected from the cold, enjoying companionship rather than the booze. When the 10 o'clock drum sounds, they scurry off for supper, or more drink:

Nou some to porter, some to punch,
Some to their wife, and some their wench,
Retire, while noisy ten-hours' drum
Gars a' your trades gae dand'ring hame.
Nou mony a club, jocose an free,
Gie a' to merriment an glee:
Wi sang an glass, they fley the pouer
O care that wad harrass the hour:
For wine an Bacchus still bear doun
Our thrawart fortune's wildest froun:
It maks you stark, an bauld, an brave,
E'en whan descending to the grave.

From *Auld Reekie* Robert Fergusson

When Robert Burns arrived in Edinburgh in 1786, he set out to pay his respects to the poet he called 'my elder brother in muse'. Specific poems show Fergusson's influence, but it was the comic spirit, the racy language, the ability to mock pomposity and pretension Burns admired and reflected. Fergusson's poems are about the world he knew. He was not in the least interested in appearing literary or genteel. In the Edinburgh of the early 1770s, he was as unfashionable as it was possible to be; the city was concerned with building the New Town while the literati discussed James Macpherson's effusions.

Burns was astonished to find Fergusson buried in an unmarked grave. He applied to the town council and received permission to remedy the matter.

Stewart Conn reckons Fergusson didn't fit into the accepted notions of speech: 'He was too close to what was under the burgers of Edinburgh's noses but they weren't willing to let their eyes drop to it. Burns' regard for him I'm sure was heightened in conjunction with admiration for the poetry by awareness of the social hobnail boot that was planted on Fergusson.'

Burns fashioned Scots into a voice of the people, which has endured to the present day. In doing so he provided a body of work whose quality is recognised across the world. His powers of observation and ability to extract a universal truth from the mundane are unequalled. And he does it in a language many of his contemporaries were anxious to lose and which many still find common:

> O wad some Power the giftie gie us
> To see oursels as ithers see us!
> It wad frae monie a blunder free us
>   An' foolish notion:
> What airs in dress an' gait wad lea'e us,
> An' ev'n devotion!

From To a Louse Robert Burns

The problems of Scots were compounded for Gaelic. For anyone from the Gaeltachd, life was elsewhere. My parents and grandparents are buried in Pennyfuir Cemetery, Oban. I go there maybe once or twice a year. And every time it seems to me the story of Gaelic can be told in about half a dozen steps. Exile obviously contributed to Gaelic's decline, but people thought the language was useless, that the future lay with English. My grandfather was a native Gaelic speaker who spoke virtually no English. His grave's on the opposite side of the path, a few steps away from my father's grave. He was bilingual. Neither my children nor I speak Gaelic.

Gaelic now has European minority language status with fewer than sixty thousand speakers. My relationship to Gaelic, like many others and also like many people's relationship to Scots, is neither immediate nor accessible, but it's still there in the background for all of us.

> He who loses his language loses his world. The
> Highlander who loses his language loses his world.
> The space ship that goes astray among planets loses the
>   world.
> In an orange world how would you know orange? In
> a world without evil how would you know good?

From Shall Gaelic Die? Iain Crichton Smith

Writers usually have one voice and write in a single language. Iain Crichton Smith was nothing short of a phenomenon, producing novels, stories, poems, plays, essays, journalism of extraordinary veracity and quality in both Gaelic and English. Sorley MacLean called Iain's imaginative and creative fertility 'the wonder of literary Scotland'.

His friend, Stewart Conn, is not the only writer to marvel at Iain's abilities, all the more remarkable when one considers the tug between Gaelic and English. 'With Iain it's almost like spontaneous combustion, it's almost Mozartian; it's as though he's making an electric shortcut, or a leap from one phrase to another.'

Iain Crichton Smith is one of Scotland's greatest poets and novelists. He had an international reputation as a poet before turning to fiction. His first novel *Consider the Lilies* is set in Strathnaver, and is the story of an old woman who is cleared from her cottage by Patrick Sellar. Resisting the break-up of the world she has known, she is betrayed by her church and sheltered by a free-thinking stonemason.

These were themes Iain explored in his poetry. His work explores individual freedom and identity, especially freedom from a past that continually threatens to overwhelm and engulf the present. He constantly questions his own abilities, is tormented by the ideas of not being good enough for the difficult business of life, and confronts his characters with moral choices and dilemmas, which are answered unsatisfactorily or with exile.

Physical and mental exile, real and imagined, obsessed him. Born in Glasgow, he was raised in Lewis and lived most of his life in Oban and Taynuilt. The dilemmas his characters face often result in a loss of faith, or they are struggling to make sense of their faith. The individual seems separated from the community, something we find runs through twentieth-century Scottish fiction. With Iain it's much more. It isn't that the community doesn't care; they are often a mean-spirited lot, antagonistic and smug.

Yet, he is capable of finding warmth and humour, of looking at the world with a surreal perspective which dictates its own logic and is vastly entertaining. It is extraordinary to find a writer who can turn his wheelie-bin into a Grecian urn while marvelling at the 'spendthrift universe':

A night such as we have never known,
millions of stars, shooting stars, a moon.
I stand and breathe the sky. It is breathing.
The supernatural light rests on the bin.

From *Putting out the Ashes* Iain Crichton Smith

Or can produce such bizarre, tragi-comic fiction as *Murdo*, a would-be writer who philosophises on how a herring and a potato came to be on the same plate and ponders what significant lessons can be drawn. Iain Crichton Smith lampoons the preachers whose banalities he had to endure along with the would-be philosophers who are interested only in their own wit and wisdom. He finds grace and joy in eccentricity, marvels at the ordinary and is never less than astonished by the possibilities of human endurance.

If the influence or importance of Scottish literature outweighs the size of the country, its history and population, then, within Scotland, the same can be said of Gaelic. The language has produced a body of writers whose work and influence reaches far beyond the Gaeltachd:

I dreamt I was the seafloor
and you were the weight of the ocean pressing down on me
your quiet words of love in my ears
now and again, golden elegant and strange
like seahorses, like grace notes, tiny floating saxophones.

From *Seahorses* Kevin MacNeil

Kevin MacNeil recognises Gaelic's plight with an emotion that cuts through intellectual or political debate. 'I think sometimes of Gaelic being a very much beloved friend or relative, or partner who's perhaps in hospital and that some doctors are being slightly pessimistic, and saying well, shouldn't we just pull the plug? But if you love that person of course you want the doctors to do everything within their powers, regardless of money, regardless of bigoted comments other people might make, you want that person to survive, and to survive as strongly and powerfully as possible far, far into the future.'

In the early years of the twentieth century the language debate took a new turn. From a garden shed in Montrose the revival that was to become known as the Scottish Literary Renaissance began. This was where Christopher Murray Grieve reinvented himself as Hugh MacDiarmid.

The shed survives. I visited it on a sunny day that was only disturbed by children playing on a quiet council street. Neither the shed's owner nor his next-door neighbour had heard of Hugh MacDiarmid.

As a writer and polemicist he addressed social and political issues directly. His use of language was a political act and the way he used the language to achieve a new directness and potency, addressing both the sublime and the vulgar, was something no Scot had considered since Burns.

The lyrics in his first two collections of poems *Sangschaw*, published in 1925, and *Penny Wheep*, published a year later dragged Scots into the twentieth century, combining the language of the ballads with modern imagery which unfolds line upon line.

A Drunk Man Looks at the Thistle, also published in 1926, is a lengthy dramatic monologue packed with optimism at a time when others saw failure and spiritual decline, when the western world was trying to come to terms with the possibility of economic collapse, something MacDiarmid as a Communist felt was both inevitable and welcome. Where others saw futility, MacDiarmid produced a poem which carries itself beyond national identity, urging acceptance of the mystery of existence:

The language that but sparely flooers
And maistly gangs to weed;
The thocht o' Christ and Calvary
Aye liddenin' in my heid;
And a' dour provincial thocht
That merks the Scottish breed
– These are the thistle's characters,
To argie there's nae need.
Hoo weel my verse embodies
The thistle you can read!
– But will a Scotsman never
Frae this vile growth be freed?

From *A Drunk Man Looks
at the Thistle* Hugh MacDiarmid

Among other themes the poem explores, especially in the early section, are Scotland's loss of identity, loss of language and belief in itself. Yet the poem also examines the mysteries of existence. MacDiarmid investigates the potential of human existence, eventually returning to consider the future of Scotland, something which is viewed with horror when the Drunk Man considers his companions on the Great Wheel: Harry Lauder and John Knox, Burns and Mary, Queen of Scots. The poem combines an intense spirituality with a socialist ideal, themes that were to occupy most of his life and work.

The poet Liz Niven loves the poem's achievement: 'Like the drunk man it staggers, it moves around geographically, intellectually, emotionally. He moves the thistle as an emblem, as a symbol for nationhood, and for the personal element of what identity means to him. It's an amazing piece of work linguistically and the only example at that time of Scots being used in such a masterly fashion.'

MacDiarmid's most extraordinary achievement was to create a new language. He saw Lallans as the route to Scotland's linguistic future. 'He invented himself,' says Jackie Kay, 'and he invented a language to go with it; and these little lyric poems he wrote are absolutely beautiful.'

MacDiarmid saw a huge creative potential in the Scots language and using Jamieson's *Scots Dictionary* as his principle source produced a series of deceptive lyrics which initially appear to be pure poetry, but generate intense cosmological statements.

I met ayont the cairney
A lass wi toosie hair
Singin' till a bairnie
That was nae langer there.

Winds wi warlds to swing
Dinnae sing sae sweet,
The licht that bends owre a' thing
Is less ta'en up wi't.

From *Empty Vessel* Hugh MacDiarmid

George Bruce traced the origins of this poem to 'Jenny Nettles', a song in David Herd's *Ancient and Modern Scottish Songs*. Alan Bold called it, '. . . one of MacDiarmid's most intricate lyrics, a poem that spans the centuries by interpreting a Scottish folk song in the light of modern scientific supposition'.

Liz Niven finds the poem 'just so beautiful. And it's accessible. So much is condensed in just those few lines.'

And William McIlvanney finds MacDiarmid's lyrics almost magical: 'It's like a necromancer who makes a language that appears to be dead breathe again.'

'To write poetry you really need to get into those essential words of a language,' says Matthew Fitt. 'And they're all there waiting, hiding, left gathering dust in various dictionaries, they're all waiting for folk to come and pick them up and use them again.'

MacDiarmid was expelled from the Scottish National Party for his Communism and also from the Communist Party of Great Britain for his nationalism. He abandoned Scots for English when he seemed to have won success and followers, was a man of great kindness, intelligence and charm who conducted feuds over decades and was extraordinarily vain, even for a writer. Norman MacCaig said he was

> . . . mild as milk, he'd charm old ladies up
> on to the mantelpiece – and leave them there.
> From *Hugh MacDiarmid* Norman MacCaig

'His aim,' says Stewart Conn, 'was nothing less than to witness and be at the centre of the regeneration of the whole spectrum of Scottish life and culture, particularly in terms of language to have the Scottish tongue regenerated and used, and to pick up the threads of Scottish literature.'

And for Edwin Morgan: 'His main importance was a tremendous breakthrough in the 1920s. Poetry was in the doldrums in Scotland until that time, and whatever one thinks about his work in detail, he made a great breakthrough. He was the axe that split the wood, and that was very important.'

He breathed ambition and self-confidence into the literary scene and maybe even into the country itself. In so doing, he influenced a generation of writers who did not simply choose to write poetry, but elected to do so in Lallans.

His influence is still around. Matthew Fitt was inspired by MacDiarmid to write a science fiction novel in Lallans. *But n Ben A-Go-Go* is the story of a futuristic Scotland mostly sunk under water by floods and ravaged by a HIV-like virus called Senga:

Fitt's intentions were to use the language in the same way as MacDiarmid. 'Folk had been telling me since I was a wee lad that Scots was simply for grannies, it was for the past, it was for folk who lived in a Highland hame somewhere and not relevant to the present and certainly nothing to do with the future and I just thought that idea was complete mince.'

Irvine Welsh reckons Fitt is 'making a statement that it's not necessarily a language of the past, it can be a language of the future as well. A clever thing to do, a science fiction book in a language that's supposed to be extinct.'

Yet implicit in Fitt's novel is an acknowledgement that the debate is far from won. It carries an Introduction in English telling folk how to read the book.

In the 1960s Tom Leonard reopened the language debate. Leonard followed his voice, saw language as a political issue and began to re-examine the split between language of the intellect and language of the heart.

its thi lang-
wij a thi
guhtr thaht hi
said its thi
langwij a
thi guhtr

awright fur
funny stuff
ur
Stanley Bax-
ter ur but
luv n science
n thaht naw

thi langwij
a thi
intillect hi
said thi lang-
wij a thi intill-
ects Inglish

then whin thi
doors slid

oapn hi raised
his hat geen
mi a fare-
well nod flung
oot his right

fit bodly n
fell eight
storeys
doon thi
empty
lift shaft

From *Unrelated Incidents* Tom Leonard

The notion that there was such a thing as a standardised Scots was challenged. It simply did not accord with urban experience, and writers could find little difference between an English teacher who told them to speak English without a Scots accent and linguistic purists who favoured Scots without an urban accent.

Leonard challenges the dictum and authority of Received Pronunciation, as well as the political assumptions behind it. There are, he argues, hidden assumptions of power in the ways we speak and perceive language. This further impoverishes the victims of establishment power, combating the authority of the voice.

'Tom Leonard's got a wonderful poem,' says Liz Lochhead, 'which starts off – "And the prisons were full of many voices, but never the dialect of the judges." It probably says more about the power systems inherent in language than just about anything else.'

When James Kelman won the Booker Prize in 1994, there was an obvious hostility among the media and literary establishment, a sense of outrage that a novel which clearly celebrates the language of the street should merit such a prize. It is difficult not to see their objections as simple snobbery, especially since they fail to address, far less appreciate, the central point; the right of writers to claim the English language as a legitimate means of expressing their experience in a voice that is also central to that experience.

This is the insistence of self-expression, which is not exactly unknown. American writers have been using this technique at least since the 1930s and, as far as Scottish literature is concerned, something similar is found in the stories of James Hogg and the works of Lewis Grassic Gibbon. The idea of a narrator using natural speech rhythms and accents to relate the narrative as well as the dialogue isn't unknown in English literature. In all these instances, of course, the accent is different.

The argument can be nothing but political when it is compounded with notions of class and privilege. In most novels and stories written about working-class characters, the assumption is that the voice of the omnipotent author is absolute. He or she can enter the mind of the character and tell the reader what the character is thinking, and, by adopting the role of narrator, can appear superior to the character and reader simultaneously. Similarly, punctuation which separates dialogue from the narrative automatically isolates the dialogue, making the authorial voice more important.

The issue at hand seems not to be construction or debasement of linguistic standards, as if linguistic standards had been an absolute. It's the swearing; the language certain characters use is atrocious.

The argument hinges on a value system; what is good and bad language? The repetition of certain words not only mirrors the ways in which they are generally used, but also reduces their impact. It underlines the inherent point, that it's not the words themselves which are offensive, rather it's their context. It's the ways in which they are used. There are a number of writers who reserve the right to use language in this way.

Not that the argument convinces everyone. Ian Rankin remembers showing James Kelman's first novel *The Busconductor Hines* to his father: 'I thought, Oh, my dad's gonnae love this, he's a working-class guy and this is as much about his kindae life as about this bus conductor. So I took it home to him; and he said, "I can't read this pal. It's not written in English." I looked at the books my dad read; a working-class Scottish guy and he read spy novels and thrillers, and they were all written in standard English. What he did was put his own inflections into them in his head when he read. So, right from the start, I decided I would write in standard English and people could read it in whatever lilt or voice they wanted.'

There is no doubting the fact that James Kelman and Tom Leonard have broadened the linguistic debate. Their refusal to accept a linguistic value system, to see it as an extension of the class war and to deny the validity of any class-based hierarchy has pioneered change, not just in Scottish writing. A new generation of writers has accepted the freedoms, none more successfully than Irvine Welsh.

Ah soon started tae feel fucking shan n aw. Bad cramps wir beginning tae hit us as we mounted the stairs tae Johnny's gaff. Ah wis dripping like a saturated sponge, every step bringing another gush fae ma pores. Sick Boy was probably even worse, but the cunt was beginning no tae exist fir us. Ah wis only aware ay him slouching tae a halt oan the banister in front ay us, because he wis blocking ma route tae Johnny's and the skag. He wis struggling fir breath, haudin grimly oantay the railing, looking as if he wis gaunnae spew intae the stairwell.

– Awright Si? ah sais irritably, pissed off at the cunt fir haudin us up.

From *Trainspotting* Irvine Welsh

When *Trainspotting* was published Welsh was 'portrayed as a strange creature schooled in darkness'. This politicised his thinking. 'The response to what I'd done showed me it was political,' he said.

The classroom was the place where Scots and Gaelic were

hammered out of us, where we were told to sit up straight and
speak properly.

Oh saying it was one thing
but when it came to writing it
in black and white
the way it had to be said
was as if you were posh, grown-up, male, English and dead.
> From *Kidspoem/Bairnsang* Liz Lochhead

It goes without saying that the survival of these languages has to
start in school. Nor can it be confined. We have to work with what
we've got rather than impose standards or norms. It was in
primary school William McIlvanney realised he spoke a strange
language. 'When I went to primary school,' he says, 'the social
workers of the word arrived, and re-papered the house with
English.'

And though the poet Kathleen Jamie now works in a university,
she has to go home to hear Scots spoken: 'Sometimes the Scots
language is aesthetically necessary and it's wonderful to have an
extra range. I like Scots 'cause I find it very intimate, it's very
close, close to the ear. So for small intimate poems I like the Scots.
I can't declaim in it like MacDiarmid did. Maybe it's just a
childhood thing, 'cause that's when I heard it, when things were
small and close. It's a lovely language to work in, you know. If I
ever have two or three years to spare I'd like to bring it up to
speed; it's a kind of stunted, retarded thing at the minute, but it's
nice to work in and you've got to do it now and again to keep it
alive, keep it fresh. It's a bonnie language. I'd like to hear more of
it. It's like seeing a rare bird or something, to hear a wonderful
phrase in Scots.'

I say her phrases to myself
In my head
Or under the shallows of my breath,

Restful shapes moving.
The day and ever. The day and ever.

The train this slow evening
Goes down England
Browsing for the right sky,
Too blue swapped for a cool grey.
For miles I have been saying
What like is it
The way I say things when I think.
Nothing is silent. Nothing is not silent.
What like is it.

Only tonight
I am happy and sad
Like a child
Who stood at the end of summer
And dipped a net
In a green, erotic pond. *The day
And ever. The day and ever.*
I am homesick, free, in love
With the way my mother speaks.

The Way My Mother Speaks Carol Ann Duffy

Travellers' Tales

When they reached the new land they rebuilt the old one,
they called the new mountains by old names,
they carved a Presbyterian church on the hill
>   From *When They Reached the New Land*
>   Iain Crichton Smith

Something like thirty million people across the world claim Scottish descent, making humanity one of our biggest exports. Not all our émigrés were forced. Some chose to go. And just as Scotland has always evoked a romantic, even mysterious image in the minds of those who came here, so many of our writers have been drawn to the world beyond our borders.

Many leave for economic reasons; others are driven by a spirit of adventure. Some find freedoms they cannot get here and all take an idea of Scotland with them, which is further informed by what they experience. Their journeys have enriched our literature, allowing several writers to claim a place on the world stage.

None was a travel writer as such, though some have obviously written about travel. For most, the journey was a search, a bid for adventure and ultimately a fresh way of seeing the familiar. But travel involves the concept of separate places, the place we are leaving and the one we are going to; and travellers often inhabit both places simultaneously, carrying the place they are leaving with them as an imaginative entity. And if it does present the familiar in a new way, do we have to leave to see ourselves clearly?

Alexander McCall Smith, whose highly successful series *The No. 1 Ladies' Detective Agency* has an African setting, is in no doubt: 'Travel enables you to see things for what they are because you're able to compare and you are perhaps more able to understand why things are different. So it means you're less likely to accept the assumptions that go with a place. It liberates you.'

Irvine Welsh agrees. Travel lets you see the familiar in a new light. 'I think when you're brought up somewhere you think, this place is really mundane, and you cannae wait to get out, to be somewhere else. Now I see Scotland as one of the most exotic, strangest places in the world. The more I've travelled and the more places I've been to, I just see how crazy Scotland is compared to other places.'

Grey recumbent tombs of the dead in desert places.
Standing stones on the vacant wine-red moor,
Hills of sheep, and the homes of silent, vanquished races,
And winds austere and pure:

Be it granted to me to behold you again in dying,
Hills of home! And to hear again the call;
Hear about the graves of the martyrs the peewees crying,
And hear no more at all.

From *To S.R. Crockett* Robert Louis Stevenson

Robert Louis Stevenson's feelings about Scotland are at best ambivalent, especially in exile. His dewy-eyed expressions of longing are mainly for the Highlands. His dominant memories of Edinburgh are of the climate, hardly surprising since he longed for a more amenable environment.

Edinburgh pays cruelly for her high seat in one of the vilest climates under heaven. She is liable to be beaten upon by all the winds that blow, to be drenched with rain, to be buried in cold sea fogs out of the east, and powdered with the snow as it comes flying southward from the Highland hills. The weather is raw and boisterous in winter, shifty and ungenial in summer, and a downright meteorological purgatory in the spring. The delicate die early, and I, as a survivor, among bleak winds and plumping rain, have been sometimes tempted to envy them their fate. For all who love shelter and the blessings of the sun, who hate dark weather and perpetual tilting against squalls, there could scarcely be found a more unhomely and harassing place of residence. Many such aspire angrily after that Somewhere-else of the imagination, where all troubles are supposed to end. They lean over the great bridge which joins the New Town with the Old – that windiest spot, or high altar, in this northern temple of the winds – and watch the trains smoking out from under them and vanishing into the tunnel on a voyage to brighter skies. Happy the passengers who shake off the dust of Edinburgh, and have heard for the last time the cry of the east wind among her chimney-tops! And yet the place establishes an interest in people's hearts; go where they will, they find no city of the same distinction; go where they will, they take a pride in their old home.

From *Edinburgh: Picturesque Notes*
Robert Louis Stevenson

The weather had a crucial effect on his health; and despite his sentimental attachment to Edinburgh, he couldn't wait to be off. But travel was more than a means of escape. Stevenson was restless to find what he couldn't identify, and his search for the mysterious gave him a language, it gave him a voice. As a writer, his reputation has never been higher: 'Stevenson continues to grow,' says Candia McWilliam. 'His star is increasingly in the ascendant. He's there for good.'

'Travel's everything to Stevenson,' says Chris Dolan. 'It's what he wrote about from the word go; and I think it's at the heart of everything he did, the idea of "the other", of travelling to the other and beyond, to travelling into the other person inside yourself. So no matter where he goes, he's always looking for the other person.'

As a child, long periods of illness transformed Stevenson's sick bed into a raft for his imagination, taking him on fantastic journeys, firstly into the Edinburgh outside his window and eventually into worlds beyond. The folds of his sheets became snowfields or distant mountain ranges. Streetlights shone like distant galaxies. Later in life, still labouring under the weight of sickness, Stevenson would take to his bed to continue his creative journey.

> And sometimes sent my ships in fleets
> All up and down among the sheets;
> Or brought my trees and houses out,
> And planted cities all about.
>
> From *The Land of Counterpane*
> Robert Louis Stevenson

Donna Tartt's novel *The Little Friend* is set in small-town Mississippi, where Harriet grows up in her brother's shadow. He was murdered when she was a baby. The murder remains unsolved and her family have never recovered. Harriet is steeped in Stevenson's adventure stories, along with Kipling and Conan Doyle, and decides to solve the murder and exact her revenge. Donna Tartt was introduced to Stevenson by her Scots grandmother, who read to her as a child.

'*Kidnapped* and *Treasure Island* were the books that made me into a writer,' she says. 'I think, because they made me preoccupied with the kinds of questions writers ask: why do good people act foolishly sometimes? If all people are a mixture of good and bad then at what point is the line crossed, at what point does the good person become bad, and at what point is the bad person able to redeem themselves [sic]? How far can you go, and still come back, which, of course, is the great question of *Dr Jekyll and Mr Hyde*.'

When she was writing *The Little Friend*, she had a picture of Stevenson on the wall beside her desk: 'Stevenson is an inspiration in so many ways. Even in the very mundane sense of going to one's desk, and feeling a bit tired, you think of poor Stevenson's suffering and suddenly the day's work doesn't seem so bad. Apart from being a great stylist, and a great storyteller, and all the things we take for granted, he has such a lightness of touch, his psychology is astounding and he's a great writer of the supernatural; actually he's one of the greatest writers in the English language.'

The journey is the oldest and purest narrative structure. Its simplicity and directness, its changing landscapes and characters offer a ready-made medium for a writer to explore and use imaginatively. The hero sets out in the beginning with a goal and after many adventures reaches his destination having been changed in some way. It's been the template for yarns from *The Odyssey* to road movies.

As a young man, the inspiration of real journeys through real landscapes earned Stevenson his first money as a writer and gained him a reputation. 'He goes abroad to get in touch with a kind of bohemian idea,' says Chris Dolan, 'to get away from the professional middle class and to become something bigger and wilder and more romantic. One of the reasons he's such a great writer is that he never quite loses the proto-Calvinist, middle-class person, the Edinburgh person within him.'

Wounded in love, Stevenson trekked across southern France in 1878, with a fiercely independent and obstinate donkey called Modestine. But even here, Scotland was never far away.

It was Sabbath; the mountain fields were all vacant in the sunshine; and as we came down through St Martin de Frugeres, the church was crowded to the door, there were people kneeling without upon the steps and the sound of the priest's chanting came forth out of the dim interior. It gave me a home feeling on the spot; for I am a countryman of the Sabbath, so to speak, and all Sabbath observances, like a Scottish accent, strike in me mixed feelings, grateful and the reverse.

From *Travels with a Donkey* Robert Louis Stevenson

The most baffling, surprising and ultimately thrilling aspect of Stevenson is his range. It is difficult to imagine how *Treasure Island* and *Kidnapped* came from the writer who created *Dr Jekyll and Mr Hyde*. And though it was written early in his career, *Travels with a Donkey* shows yet another side of Stevenson, a side separate from the adventurer or psychological realist. It discloses an observant wanderer, a travel writer who shares his surprise at what he finds and returns delighted, with new ways of seeing.

Stevenson was obviously aware that travellers' tales can make great stories, so it's no coincidence that many of his later novels are structured round a journey.

Kidnapped is a tale of murder and political intrigue, mostly set against the backdrop of the Highlands in the aftermath of the 1745 Jacobite Rebellion. Two fugitives, Alan Breck Stewart and David Balfour, both righteous men, flee into exile in their own land. For David Balfour, the book's narrator, his flight through the heather reveals an exotic world, a Scotland so different from what he has known as to be utterly foreign.

Sometimes we walked, sometimes ran; and as it drew on to morning, walked ever less and ran the more. Though, upon its face, that country appeared to be a desert, yet there were huts and houses of the people, of which we must have passed more than twenty, hidden in quiet places of the hills . . . For all our hurry, day began to come in while we were still far from any shelter. It found us in a prodigious valley, strewn with rocks and where ran a foaming river. Wild mountains stood around it; there grew there neither grass nor trees; and I have sometimes thought since then, that it may have been the valley called Glencoe, where the massacre was in the time of King William. But for the details of our itinerary, I am all to seek; our way lying now by short cuts, now by great detours; our pace being so hurried; our time of journeying

usually by night; and the names of such places as I asked
and heard, being in the Gaelic tongue and the more easily
forgotten.

From *Kidnapped* Robert Louis Stevenson

The novelist Val McDermid finds David Balfour's journey very
revealing: 'To an English person, or an American person, it's the
same country. But, of course, a Scot recognises a huge difference, a
gulf between the Highlands and the Lowlands, particularly at the
time when *Kidnapped* is set. Family was set against family,
depending on where they came from and with what sept of the
clan their allegiances lay.'

For the priggish David Balfour, it's a journey of discovery. Not
only does he see the country in the company of a pock-faced
adventurer as different from himself as it's possible to be, apart
from mutual vanities and pride, he learns appearances can be
misleading, finds generosity, loyalty and courage which not only
run counter to his Uncle Ebeneezer's behaviour, but have generally been beyond his understanding. In *Kidnapped*, Stevenson
was re-stating an obvious, personal belief, which was clearly based
on his experience; by travel we discover as much about ourselves as
we do about the world outside.

Kidnapped was written while Stevenson's precarious health left
him exiled in Bournemouth. Despite his health, he was to spend
most of his adult life as a wanderer, travelling to Canada, America
and Australia, and eventually settling as far from Edinburgh as was
possible for Victorian Britain to imagine on the island of Upolu in
Samoa in the South Pacific. From here he gained a new perspective. His writing began to challenge the country he left behind and
to question its values.

'He came to understand the world much more fully in a political
sense from what he saw in the South Seas and from South Sea
islanders,' says Val McDermid. 'He understood much more about
the way people work, about political systems, than he did living in
Scotland or even travelling in Europe. He became much more

conscious of the duality, the impact of one culture on another. All of this is very clear in his writings.'

By the end of the nineteenth century a quarter of the world was ruled by the British Empire. Given the yearning for romance and action heroes, it's not surprising that *Treasure Island* and *Kidnapped* conquered readers across the world. But Stevenson was no propagandist, and the Empire he criticised was the same British Empire that made his travels possible and allowed his books to have such a wide audience. It's difficult to imagine how Scottish writing might have fared without this connection. The Empire brought a bigger world to Scotland.

'I think that without Empire, Scottish culture generally would have been different,' says Chris Dolan. 'The whole idea of Britain being at the centre of this massive spread of countries across the world opens up the world at home to all sorts of possibilities.'

Sir Arthur Ignatius Conan Doyle was a true son of the Empire. A doctor of medicine and adventurer, knighted in 1902 for his loyalty to king and country and his work in Boer War propaganda, he is best remembered for his extraordinary creation, the eccentric and brilliant Sherlock Holmes. Conan Doyle wasn't the first to write detective fiction, but he provided a matrix and gave the form its most memorable character.

Though by far the most popular writer of his time, until 1990 no anthology of Scottish writing included work by Sir Arthur Conan Doyle. Few surveys even contain his name. A recent 1,269-page study of Scottish literature, with three respected academic editors and half a dozen editorial assistants, published by Edinburgh University Press, doesn't even mention him in an index which includes Erroll Flynn, Sigmund Freud, Immanuel Kant and Carole Lombard.

'There wouldn't be a tradition of crime writing, the way there is now, on either side of the Atlantic or anywhere in Europe, if it hadn't been for Conan Doyle,' says Val McDermid.

Conan Doyle is one of a number of Scottish writers who follow a trail blazed by Burns, Scott, Hogg, Galt, Stevenson, Jane Porter,

Joanna Baillie and even Lord George Byron; writers who have exported a sense of Scotland, or whose work has trailed a vision of Scotland and Scottish culture in its wake. Fewer writers exemplify Scottish writing's international status better than Conan Doyle. He created an immediately recognisable symbol, which few associate with Scotland, yet all the connections are there.

Conan Doyle was born in Picardy Place at the top of Leith Walk, Edinburgh, in 1859, into a family of ten children, struggling against poverty and their father's alcoholism. He was devoted to his mother. It was from her he got his love of storytelling, a passion he would develop as a medical student at Edinburgh University, where he rubbed shoulders with Stevenson and J.M. Barrie, with whom he later collaborated. Nine years younger than Stevenson, they both shared an admiration for the stories of Emile Gaboriau, inventor of the French detective novel, and a liking for Rutherford's Bar.

Few Doyle stories are set in Scotland, though it seems clear his Edinburgh medical training and memory of the place itself played an important part in the creation of Holmes and his world. Holmes' deductive powers were based on Conan Doyle's teacher, Dr Joseph Bell, whose character is also reflected in one of Doyle's other creations, Professor Challenger. And while 'Scotch' characters occur in his other work, notably the Brigadier Gerard stories he wrote in an attempt to replace Holmes in the public's affection, Edinburgh, medicine and Rutherford's Bar come together in *The Last Operation*.

Like J.M. Barrie, Doyle could present England to the English with a detachment that hid sharper contours and was often more recognisable than native versions; something which is, if anything, even more evident in the works of another cultural migrant, John Buchan.

The Sherlock Holmes stories have been translated into more than fifty languages, made into plays, films, radio and television series, a musical comedy, a ballet, cartoons, comic books, and advertisements. By 1920 Doyle was one of the most highly paid writers in the world.

'This is indeed a mystery,' I remarked. 'What do you imagine that it means?'

'I have no data yet. It is a capital mistake to theorise before one has data. Insensibly one begins to twist facts to suit theories, instead of theories to suit facts . . .'

From *A Scandal in Bohemia* Sir Arthur Conan Doyle

Conan Doyle was born with a passion for travel and when, at the age of twenty, he was given the chance to sign on board a whaler, he seized the opportunity. He later did a similar term in Africa, experiences he drew on for his Professor Challenger stories, but the Arctic adventure stayed with him. He later wrote that he thrilled to the chase of the whale and loved the matiness of the crew. The Arctic 'awakened the soul of a born wanderer', he wrote. 'I went on board the whaler a big straggling youth and came off a powerful man.'

He was standing upon the bridge about an hour ago, peering as usual through his glass, while I was walking up and down the quarterdeck. The majority of the men were below at their tea, for the watches have not been regularly kept of late. Tired of walking, I leaned against the bulwarks, and admired the mellow glow cast by the sinking sun upon the great ice fields which surround us. I was suddenly aroused from the reverie into which I had fallen by a hoarse voice at my elbow, and starting round I found that the Captain had descended and was standing by my side. He was staring out over the ice with an expression in which horror, surprise, and something approaching to joy were contending for the mastery. In spite of the cold, great drops of perspiration were coursing down his forehead, and he was evidently fearfully excited. His limbs twitched like those of a man upon the verge of an epileptic fit, and the lines about his mouth were drawn and hard.

'Look!' he gasped, seizing me by the wrist, but still keeping his eyes upon the distant ice, and moving his head slowly in a horizontal direction, as if following some object which was moving across the field of vision. 'Look! There, man, there! Between the hummocks! Now coming out from behind the far one! You see her – you must see her! There still! Flying from me, by God, flying from me – and gone!'

From *The Captain of the Pole Star* Sir Arthur Conan Doyle

When Conan Doyle eventually graduated as a doctor in 1881 he drew a cartoon of himself captioned 'Licensed to Kill'. He practised as an eye specialist at Southsea, near Portsmouth, for ten years before becoming a full-time writer. His first novel, *A Study in Scarlet*, was an instant success. Published in 1887, it introduced the world to Sherlock Holmes and his loyal friend Dr Watson. Together they were a sensation. Doyle followed with *The Sign of Four* and in 1891 *The Adventures of Sherlock Holmes* was incrementally published in *Strand* magazine

But Doyle came to hate his creation. Sherlock Holmes cramped his style. He wanted to be seen as more than a writer of commercial fiction and had such little respect for Holmes eventually that he told another writer, 'You may marry him, murder him or do what you like with him. I don't care.'

By 1893 he devised Holmes' death in *The Final Problem*, which was published in the December issue of *Strand*. Holmes meets Moriarty at the Reichenbach Falls in Switzerland and disappears. Watson finds a letter from Homes, stating, 'I have already explained to you, however, that my career had in any case reached its crisis, and that no possible conclusion to it could be more congenial to me than this.'

Some readers wore mourning bands and *Strand* lost 20,000 subscriptions, despite Doyle going out of his way to create the dashing Napoleonic hero, Brigadier Gerard. Then, in *The Hound of the Baskervilles*, published in 1902, Doyle narrated what he claimed was one of the dead detective's earlier cases, which only increased public demand. Holmes' role as the world's favourite lawman seemed assured and Doyle resurrected him the following year in *The Empty House.*

> I moved my head to look at the cabinet behind me. When I turned again Sherlock Holmes was standing smiling at me across my study table. I rose to my feet, stared at him for some seconds in utter amazement, and then it appears that I must have fainted for the first and last time in my life.
>
> From *The Empty House* Sir Arthur Conan Doyle

'That's a lesson for all of us who write about a series detective,' says Ian Rankin. 'At what point do you decide to jack it in, and will the public let you? Are you willing to take the risk of writing books that are less successful, just because you're bored of your character? For a lot of us, Conan Doyle's an object lesson in what you can and can't do as a writer.'

Conan Doyle seems to have made a conscious effort to shed his Scottishness when he moved south. But his background seeped through. Holmes' intelligent deductions were obviously part of the entertainment. But there's a subversive quality to Holmes. He doesn't share his secrets, has boundless nervous energy and a capacity for deception that Edwardian Britain would have found subversively daring and implausible enough to be amusing.

On the other hand, the defence of decent British values lies at the heart of everything John Buchan wrote. Born in Perth in 1875, the son of a Free Church of Scotland minister, he is one of the most popular thriller writers of all time.

Buchan was a journalist on *The Spectator*, a barrister in Middle Temple, a partner in the publishing company of Thomas Nelson & Son, Unionist candidate for Peebles and Selkirk, war correspondent for *The Times*, a major in the Intelligence Corps, Director of Information and Director of Intelligence at the Ministry of Information, a Director, then Chairman of Reuters, MP for Scottish Universities, High Commissioner to the General Assembly of the

Church of Scotland, first Baron Tweedsmuir and Governor-General of Canada.

His writing was equally varied. He published more than one hundred books, the first while he was a student, ranging from thrillers to scholarly studies, historical fiction to biography. With Neil Munro and S.R. Crockett he forms the group of historical romancers who followed Scott and Stevenson's lead, where a dashing young protagonist, through no fault of his own, finds himself out of his depth in the midst of political, social or religious intrigue. This is a fiction, which sets social order against chaos and is generally set in the past; leaving the impression that Scotland is a settled country.

Buchan's first novel was published in 1895. His second, *John Burnet of Barnes* is in the Stevenson mould, as developed by Neil Munro. Burnet is modelled on Alan Breck Stewart and even the chapter headings are reminiscent of *Kidnapped* or Munro's *The New Road* – I Ride to the South, I Fall in with Strange Friends, and so on. Buchan lacked Scott and Stevenson's historical or psychological depth, but he knew how to entertain and used the Stevenson format in many subsequent books.

The novels he called 'shockers' are still the most popular, *The Thirty-Nine Steps* and *The Three Hostages*, or historical novels, like *Witch Wood*, which looks back to Hogg and Galt by imagining a minister combating Devil worship in his small Borders community.

As a boy in Africa, reading John Buchan formed Alexander McCall Smith's view of Scotland. 'I thought of Scotland as a rather romantic place, as many people do,' he says. 'The landscape, obviously, is a prominent element of that. And I don't think in those accounts of Scotland, the reality of urban Scotland played any part at all. This was not exactly Brigadoon, but heading in that direction.'

Buchan's adventure stories were part of the energising myth of the British Empire, the kind of stories Britain told herself as she went to sleep, fuelling the dream and reaffirming her place in the world. Buchan, like many other Scots, found the Empire attractive because of the career opportunities it promised; stability coupled with romance and adventure.

'The British Empire really was the superpower of its time, the military, political, economic superpower, and it's not surprising that Scots would have associated themselves with something which was on their doorstep, so to speak,' says Alexander McCall Smith. 'It provided all sorts of opportunities. And of course the fact that people could go off to the four corners of the earth and do all sorts of interesting things while they were there, obviously would produce literature of a particular nature, rather adventurous accounts of goings on in exotic settings.'

As a young man Buchan was a Scottish patriot who called England 'vast, menacing and cruel'. His ideas changed when he won a scholarship to Brasenose College, Oxford. Far from the romantic heart of Scotland, he fell in love with the establishment's ancient magnificence, epitomising the classic case of the Scot with an inferiority complex.

'I think he had almost a schism in his heart,' says Val McDermid, 'between the Scotland that he clearly loved and drew on and gained sustenance from and the need to be approved by the establishment.'

Buchan's views of the Empire and those who created and maintained it were by today's standards often objectionable, though they typified the attitudes of his time. Like his heroes, Buchan seems to be supporting civilisation rather than the Empire, championing his own culture rather than decrying others. And while similar apologies could be made for most racists, Buchan's case seems genuine. The struggle between the civilised and the primitive is a recurring theme throughout his fiction and his unqualified support for the poetry of Hugh MacDiarmid and his championing of the infant Scottish Renaissance movement in the face of strong reaction south of the Border, shows a burly, subversive nationalism, which is reflected in his prose.

In the aftermath of the Boer War, he sailed to South Africa as part of a government team to run the country. It was a life-changing experience, which confirmed his love of travel.

The heavy tropical scents which the rain brought out of the ground, the intense silence of the drooping mists and water laden forests, the clusters of beehive Kaffir huts in the hollows, all made up a world strange and new to the sight and yet familiar to the imagination. This was the old Africa of a boy's dream, the African Colony.

From *On the Hunter's Trail* John Buchan

'I think these books had a very strong ideological reinforcing function,' says Alexander McCall Smith. 'They portrayed the British imperial enterprise as being a civilising one, as being one in which straightforward clear-browed people went forth and did good deeds. And I suppose that made people feel a little bit better about what they were doing.'

These African experiences ran deep. Richard Hannay, the hero of Buchan's *The Thirty-Nine Steps* is a Scot raised on the high African veldt, who sees the landscape of south-west Scotland through African eyes.

The air had the queer, rooty smell of bogs, but it was as fresh as mid-ocean, and it had the strangest effect on my spirits. I might have been a boy out for a spring holiday tramp instead of a man of thirty-seven very much wanted by the police. I felt just as I used to feel when I was starting out for a big trek on a frosty morning on the high veld. If you believe me, I swung along that road whistling.

From *The Thirty-Nine Steps* John Buchan

Many people find their idea of a book comes from the film. From *Trainspotting* and *Peter Pan* to Dr Jekyll and Sherlock Holmes our impressions of many of our best-known books and the films they inspired are intimately entwined. And just as the best speech in

Trainspotting comes from the film – the one about being colonised by wankers – and Sherlock Holmes has been filmed more than any other fictional character, with more than 200 titles to his credit, few books have been overtaken by its screen doubles more than *The Thirty-Nine Steps*.

In the Conan Doyle stories Holmes doesn't wear a deerstalker nor does he ever say, 'Elementary, my dear Watson.' And though *The Thirty-Nine Steps* has been filmed three times, it's the first of them, Hitchcock's 1935 version, that's the most memorable. It takes a few liberties.

Richard Hannay becomes Canadian, the action is updated to the 1930s and Hitchcock introduces a music hall performer, Mr Memory, who holds the key to the riddle. In the book the steps are down to the sea. In the 1978 version they're up to Big Ben, where Robert Powell hangs like Harold Lloyd from the clock-face in an attempt to stop a bomb going off in the House of Commons.

In Hitchcock's film, Hannay falls in with a couple of salesman on their way to Edinburgh to display a new rubber corset. Worse still, they recite limericks, a verse form which, Hitchcock knew, would unquestionably suggest a young man from Montrose or a lady named Maud to cinema audiences.

Hannay avoids detection by getting into a clinch with Madeleine Carroll. They later spend a wet night together, handcuffed in a Highland hotel, which would never happen in a Buchan book. Not long after they meet on the train, Hannay pulls the communication cord then dices with death on the Forth Bridge; not in the book either.

There's been speculation that Hannay was based on Lord Baden Powell, a man with known African connections, an Imperialist symbol and founder of the Boy Scout Movement, or that Edmund, later Field Marshall Lord Ironside was the prototype. His other heroes had more distinct origins. Sandy Arbuthnot was largely infused with T.E. Lawrence, and, according to Buchan's wife, Sir Edward Leithen was based on Buchan himself.

After three months in the Old Country, Richard Hannay is pretty well 'disgusted with life'. An American, Scudder, tells him a lot of 'queer things' about 'Jew anarchists' who are everywhere – 'a little white-faced Jew in a bathchair with an eye like a rattlesnake . . . he is the man who is ruling the world just now, and he has his knife in the Empire of the Tsar because his aunt was outraged and his father flogged in some one-horse location on the Volga.' They've hatched a plot to pit the Russians against the Germans. Scudder, it transpires, is Captain Theophilus Digby of the 40th Gurkhas in disguise and home on leave. When he's murdered, Hannay means to find out why:

> You may think this ridiculous for a man in danger of his life, but that was the way I looked at it. I am an ordinary sort of fellow, not braver than other people, but I hate to see a good man downed, and that long knife would not be the end of Scudder if I could play the game in his place.
>
> From *The Thirty-Nine Steps* John Buchan

Buchan's mention of a Jewish world domination plot isn't in the films either. That apart, a thin veil separates us from mayhem.

Buchan is as puzzling as a writer as he was as a man. His work shows our national experience of the Empire and its cause, especially the attitudes it bred. He was aware of the role Scottish writing had played in establishing our identity, yet his own attempts had limited success and his Canadian appointment came as his health was failing.

In the end, Buchan painted himself into a corner. He was forced to believe his cause was right, that the Empire he had championed and served, its values and the ideology of its doctrines would make the world a safer, better place. Mayhem was at hand, so his heroes battled against increasing odds.

'I think Richard Hannay is very much the predecessor of James Bond and all that *Mission Impossible* stuff,' says Val McDermid. 'He's the guy who goes out there and saves the rest of us, so we can sleep easy in our beds at night because Richard Hannay is doing the business for us.'

The hero who battles against impossible odds would find its most successful champion in the works of Alistair Maclean, a brilliant thriller writer whose wonderfully crafted stories were first inspired by his experiences of war and whose books have sold more copies than any other Scot's.

Born in Glasgow, the son of a Church of Scotland minister, Maclean grew up in Daviot, Inverness-shire, speaking only Gaelic in the family home. His father died when he was fourteen, so Maclean and his mother returned to Glasgow. He left school at seventeen and a year later, in 1941, joined the Royal Navy. The call of the sea was in his blood; both his grandfathers had served before the mast and their stories thrilled him as a boy.

Maclean experienced the sea for himself during the Second World War when he served as a torpedo man in the Home, Mediterranean and Eastern Fleets. He also served on HMS *Royalist* on convoy duty in the North Atlantic. The ship was deemed a lucky one. While others were bombed, mined or torpedoed, his ship got through with nothing more than a hole in the funnel. Maclean was captured and tortured by the Japanese and he was eventually demobbed in 1946.

After the war, Maclean got an Honours degree in English at Glasgow University, and taught at Gallowfleet Secondary School. He wrote in his spare time and in 1954 he entered a *Glasgow Herald* short story competition with *The Dileas*. It won the first prize of £100:

> The *Dileas* would totter up on a wave, then, like she was falling over a cliff, smash down into the next trough with the crack of a four-inch gun, burying herself right up to the gunwales. And at the same time you could hear the fierce clatter of her screw, clawing at the thin air. Why the *Dileas* never broke her back only God knows – or the ghost of Campbell of Ardrishaig.
>
> From *The Dileas* Alistair Maclean

With encouragement from the publishers Collins, Maclean wrote his first novel, *HMS Ulysses* in 1955. Again, he drew upon the horrific scenes he'd witnessed in his time at sea; and, again, it's the story of a North Atlantic convoy during the Second World War, battling against German U-boats and foul weather.

Men on fire, human torches beating insanely at the flames that licked, scorched and then incinerated clothes, hair and skin; men flinging themselves out of the water, backs arched like tautened bows, grotesque in convulsive crucifixion; men lying dead in the water, insignificant, featureless little oil-stained mounds in an oil-soaked plain.

From *HMS Ulysses* Alistair Maclean

HMS Ulysses turned out to be one of the most successful British novels of all time and with Herman Wouk's *The Caine Mutiny* and Nicholas Monsarrat's *The Cruel Sea* is considered one of the classic navy wartime novels. Others nearer home didn't share that opinion.

A headline in the *Daily Record* screeched 'Burn It!' And a reader suggested the book 'made *Mutiny on the Bounty* look like a United Free Church of Scotland choir outing'. Maclean was unconcerned. He reckoned he'd paid the Royal Navy the greatest compliment he could.

Iain Banks loves Maclean's books: 'I think it was something about the way he handled action, the way he made his books exciting. I'm still a bit of a thriller fan and I still like a good plot, preferably with a surprise ending, and Maclean was very good at them.'

Maclean is in the *Guinness Book of Records* for writing more novels that sold over a million copies than any other author. Not surprisingly, a number of his books were turned into successful films. *Where Eagles Dare* starred Clint Eastwood and Richard Burton; *The Guns of Navarone* had a cast which included Gregory Peck, David Niven and Anthony Quinn; and *Ice-Station Zebra* featured Charles Bronson.

While John Buchan sought to defend British values, Alistair Maclean, who was writing at a time when the Empire was unravelling, simply sought to entertain and make money; which is why the biggest selling novelist of all time ended up living in Switzerland as a tax exile.

Not that all the movements have been one-way, any more than all the writers who have left Scotland have found exotic destinations. Joan Lingard, J.K. Rowling, Anne Fine and Kate Atkinson migrated inwards and live in Edinburgh. And London has as much of a pull on Scottish writers as it has done for the best part of three hundred years.

Scottish locations and concerns have found their way into Joan Lingard's, Anne Fine's and Kate Atkinson's work. And though Candia McWilliam's novel *Debatable Land* explores the old and vexed question of identity, the stories in *Wait Till I Tell You* are divided into North and South locations, and she is especially sharp on the nuances of belonging.

'I do love Edinburgh, and Edinburgh would be where, if I were given my life over again, I would live,' she says. 'It's impossible for me not to love Edinburgh because of who I am, which is the daughter of a father who gave his life to Edinburgh, and I was raised to notice every astragal, every stone, every doorstep, every shop fascia, every hole in the ground, every demolition lorry, every wrecking bull of Edinburgh, and Edinburgh's my home town, and it's next to the sea, and it's buffeted by the winds, and these are my things.'

'I'm getting more and more sad about being away from home,' she says. 'My spirit seems to reside there, and my person seems to be in the south, and it's uncomfortable having the two separated.'

Shena MacKay's work also retains its Scottish characteristics, whether she is satirising the legacy of Calvinism or the Scots' contribution to the Empire. 'She is rarely thought of as a Scot,' said Candia McWilliam, 'but she is so utterly Scots in her compassionate observations, and her very peculiar, sad, loving attention to detail.'

Like Joan Lingard, Bernard MacLaverty came to Scotland from Northern Ireland. He lived in Edinburgh and Islay before settling in Glasgow. He writes with clarity, economy and an emotional precision. Children or adolescents are often his central figures and many of his stories are based around the frailty of relationships and a need to belong. Most of his work is a response to the divisions in the Irish society he left, and division also features in the stories with a Scottish setting.

His novel *Grace Notes* not only questions one's right to absolute national identity, but also transcends both Scots and Irish experience. Catherine McKenna is a composer and unmarried mother from an Irish Catholic background who lives in Glasgow and returns to Ireland in an attempt to reconcile her position with her family and the divisions within herself. Like most of MacLaverty's work, it occupies two places simultaneously, and the divided worlds suggest place is little more than a background for working out issues of humanity. Catherine discovers aspirations rather than accomplishments. For her the journey is the process, and the stages one goes through in a quest for personal development or fulfilment are filled with endless possibilities.

Today's greatest literary exile is Muriel Spark. For my money, she is far and away our greatest living writer and should be our candidate for a Nobel Laureateship.

Muriel Spark was born in Edinburgh in 1918, where she was educated at James Gillespie's School for Girls. During the Second World War she worked for the Political Intelligence Unit and the Foreign Office. After 1949 she lived in South Africa, Rome and New York and for the last thirty years has lived in Tuscany.

Though most of her work is set outside Scotland, she is insistent on the influence her Scottish upbringing had upon her. The douce, pre-war conservative world of middle-class Edinburgh is the setting for Muriel Spark's most famous creation, the dangerously eccentric schoolmistress, Miss Jean Brodie. With this brilliant character, Spark created a literary archetype.

As they came to the end of the Meadows a group of Girl Guides came by. Miss Brodie's brood, all but Mary, walked past with eyes ahead. Mary stared at the dark blue big girls with their regimented vigorous look and broader accents of speech than the Brodie girls used when in Miss Brodie's presence. They passed, and Sandy said to Mary, 'It's rude to stare.' And Mary said, 'I wasn't staring.' Meanwhile Miss Brodie was being questioned by the girls behind on the question of the Brownies and the Girl Guides, for quite a lot of the other girls in the Junior School were Brownies.

'For those who like that sort of thing,' said Miss Brodie in her best Edinburgh voice, 'that is the sort of thing they like.'

From *The Prime of Miss Jean Brodie* Muriel Spark

'I think *The Prime of Miss Jean Brodie* is the most wonderful creation at every level,' says Alexander McCall Smith. 'It provides the most remarkable insight into the Edinburgh character and is also screamingly funny. It's a dry wit, which is appropriate for Edinburgh.'

Brodie feels restricted with life as a mistress at a girls' school, and escapes by fantasising around her own life and indoctrinating her attitudes and beliefs into the girls in her charge. Muriel Spark was living in London when she settled on the theme of the novel. Separated by time and distance from Edinburgh, she returned to her roots.

'I thought for this book I've got to get these voices in my ears,' she says. 'I've got to be there and breathing that air. I think I was right to do it, to get it right.

'Edinburgh is a kind of character in my mind, much more than any other city. It has a peculiar stamp. And there are a set of morals, a set of ideas all its own. It's very puritanical, or was; I don't know if it still is, but when I hear an Edinburgh accent I get a whiff of the morals that go with it.'

The novel was inspired by Muriel Spark's childhood memories. The book's wilful and tragic heroine was modelled on Miss

Christina Kay, her teacher at Junior School. 'She was not at all consistent,' says Muriel Spark. 'She admired Mussolini but despised the Girl Guides: "Team spirit, ridiculous!" Too artistic for that.'

Some days it seemed to Sandy that Miss Brodie's chest was flat, no bulges at all, but straight as her back. On other days her chest was breast-shaped and large, very noticeable, something for Sandy to sit and peer at through her tiny eyes while Miss Brodie on a day of lessons indoors stood erect, with her brown head held high, staring out the window like Joan of Arc as she spoke.

From *The Prime of Miss Jean Brodie* Muriel Spark

Because of her views, Spark's eponymous heroine is an exile of a sort. Miss Jean Brodie is an eccentric woman in her prime, which for her means the most visionary period of her life, 'the moment one was born for'. She has progressive views on morality and education, is separated from other teachers because of her opinions and from like-minded women by the ethos of Marcia Blane School. And while she lacks the courage to live the life she advocates, she encourages her girls to do so with some tragic results; making her, ultimately, a negative force.

'Up till this point,' says Chris Dolan, 'and by and large since that point, the idea of the broad-based Scottish education and the idea of being cultivated, in the way that only a Scot can be cultivated, is actually not a force for good, but is a force that destroys lives and makes her side with the darkest forces in Europe.'

Miss Brodie certainly shows little respect for the curriculum, but she does try to control her pupils' destinies; and part of Spark's genius is to play with time in a perfectly natural way, showing the effect Jean Brodie's teachings has on her girls. But, as with all her novels, Spark offers no solution. The moral implications are muddied. Miss Brodie is dismissed for her adoration of Mussolini and her belief in his politics. But her effect on the girls is not all bad, although often ambiguous, especially in the case of Sandy, who becomes a nun. Another girl is killed in the Spanish Civil War and the one Miss Brodie most despises later declares her school-days the happiest of her life.

In a broader sense it is possible to see Miss Brodie as a demonic figure, entirely in keeping with Spark's other creations. Scotland prides itself on its educational history, it's a defining issue for our middle classes, and to allow someone like Jean Brodie to play with impressionable minds, irrespective of the consequences, is mischievous, to say the least.

Miss Brodie believed in excellence, in *la crème de la crème* and dedicated herself to teaching her girls Art, with a capital A, which 'is greater than Science. Art comes first, and then Science,' Miss Brodie said. Edinburgh was a European capital and Scottish literature the equal of any. She would quote Hogg and Burns along with Dante and Voltaire.

They approached the Old Town which none of the girls had properly seen before, because none of their parents was so historically minded as to be moved to conduct their young into the reeking network of slums which the Old Town constituted in those years. The Canongate, The Grassmarket, The Lawnmarket were names which betokened a misty region of crime and desperation . . . It was Sandy's first experience of a foreign country, which intimates itself by its new smells and shapes and its new poor. A man sat on the icy-cold pavement; he just sat. A crowd of children, some without shoes, were playing some fight game, and some boys shouted after Miss Brodie's violet-clad company, with words that the girls had not heard before, but rightly understood to be obscene.

From *The Prime of Miss Jean Brodie* Muriel Spark

'I think of Edinburgh in a certain light,' says Muriel Spark. 'It's a pearly light, generally speaking; although it can be beautifully sunny, I always think of it in this pearly light. And with that light, it's almost a true light in my imagination, shining on truth.'

In 1961 the *New Yorker* magazine serialised *The Prime of Miss Jean Brodie* and the book became a runaway success. A Broadway play and an award-winning film followed, launching Muriel Spark onto the world stage.

'She's restless,' says Ian Rankin, 'and I like that. I like the fact that she's never found, as it were, her niche. She's not only experimental in terms of style, but she keeps finding new subjects to talk about. And that's great. I love that restlessness. I love it when people take risks.'

Now in her eighties with twenty-two novels, two biographies and several collections of short stories behind her, Muriel Spark continues to write from her home in Tuscany. But Edinburgh is never far away.

Only two novels and a few stories are set in Scotland, but she weaves references to Scott, Hogg and Stevenson into her work and one of her major themes is the supernatural, especially the effect it can have on ordinary lives. Her use of the grotesque and surreal is equally strong and ballads often provide a starting point or reference for these investigations.

The Prime of Miss Jean Brodie contains an implicit critique of teaching and the dangers implied in exposing young, impressionable minds to a charismatic influence. It also extends a frequent theme of Spark's work, a criticism of Scottish insularity and narrow-mindedness. This is something which is found in almost all her novels, but the polarity she feels about Scotland is summed up in *Symposium*, when Magnus Murchie asserts, 'Here in Scotland, people are more capable of perpetrating good or evil than anywhere else. I don't know why, but so it is.'

Murchie is by turns insane and lucid, a mentor for his niece, Margaret Damien, or Murchie, who may be a witch and murderer. Spark's fiction seems to culminate in a point of crisis where we understand where things have either gone wrong or reached a conclusion that was obvious from the beginning, generally because of a lack of individual morality, which leaves us struggling to make sense of society and find our way through the contemporary maze.

Though she famously converted to Catholicism, it is difficult to find where faith shapes her work, here or in her other novels, though if Miss Brodie is emblematic, she shows where humanity can go wrong, where our wilful ego, pride and skewed beliefs can affect the lives of others.

'I feel myself to be a Scot,' Spark says. 'I was born there, so I feel very Scottish and I still have this sense of being away from where I started. I haven't chosen any set of ideas to settle in ever. Sooner or later, I depart on certain grounds in certain ways. I call that exiledom, exiles of the heart and mind.'

POLYGON is an imprint of Birlinn Limited. Our list
includes titles by Alexander McCall Smith, Liz Lochhead,
Kenneth White, Robin Jenkins and other critically acclaimed
authors. Should you wish to be put on our catalogue
mailing list contact:

Catalogue Request
Polygon
West Newington House
10 Newington Road
Edinburgh EH9 1QS
Scotland, UK

Tel: +44 (0) 131 668 4371
Fax: +44 (0) 131 668 4466
e-mail: info@birlinn.co.uk

Postage and packing is free within the UK. For overseas
orders, postage and packing (airmail) will be charged at
30% of the total order value.

Our complete list can be viewed on our website. Go to
www.birlinn.co.uk and click on the Polygon logo at the top
of the home page.